Working From Home...

How's That Working For You?

*Clean Up Your Mess, Set Up Your Space, And
Step Up Your Productivity*

WENDY ELLIN

Sharon—
"I just want to say...
great job on your
daughter. She's the best.

Wendy

DEDICATION

This book is dedicated to all the busy professionals in the world who, in March 2020, began their "shelter-at-home" journey. In that moment, millions of people were forced to figure out how to convert their home space into their workplace. Juggling kids, pets, spouses, roommates, yard workers, neighbors, social media, breaking news reporters and WORK became the order of the day.

I trust that if the way you are working "is not working for you," this book will offer strategies, ideas, tools, tips and techniques for stepping up your productivity to enhance your work-from-home experience. You'll read stories about others doing the same thing you are: shaking your head with disbelief, making adjustments, figuring it out, all while thinking to themselves, "WTF, is this really happening?"

Uh, yes it is. So let's get to the matter of making it work. Take what you need, implement it, tweak it to work for your particular situation, and then commit to sticking with it long enough to reap the benefits.

This is not a "one size fits all." It's finding the tricks I spent 20 years perfecting as a productivity strategist, and applying them to your particular challenges of working from home. Whether it's trying to stop your son from cutting off his sister's hair just when it's your turn to present that OUT OF THE BOX idea to your boss on a Zoom call, or getting your dog to stop howling at the mosquito spray dude smack outside your front window, this, my friend, is real. This book will offer you options you may not have thought about for finding what works best for you to get what you want and need. It is meant to make you more productive, engaged in your work, and enjoying your job, all while embracing the level of crazy in your home. This pandemic has given us a unique opportunity to have it all, by eliminating our commute times and enabling us to spend more time with those we love. You just have to figure out the system that works for you. Then maybe you'll finally get what you always wanted. (As if.)

This book is the closest you may ever get to that. So grab a highlighter, throw some candy at your kids and a martini at your partner, and dig in. This one's for you.

You've got this.

ACKNOWLEDGMENTS

When I first voiced the idea of writing this book, my inner critic got real busy sharing all the reasons why that wasn't going to happen. *Who the hell are you? Haven't you already written a book? How much more wise wisdom could you possibly have to share? No one knows you. You're no authority.* Yada, yada, yada...that's the way it went inside my head. Then, as I've done for most of my adult life, I very graciously said, "Thank you for sharing," and shut her down. By the way, she never goes away, but that's another story for an entirely different book. And I'm thinking that's not mine to write.

What I realized as soon as most of the world was ordered to "shelter-in-place" was that there is about to be some major suffering going on in the world. And it had nothing to do with the coronavirus itself. The minute I saw the news on CNN that night in early March, I looked at Marty and said, "Oh my God, do you understand what this means for the majority of the world who lives among their clutter, chaos and overwhelm in their homes? You're now telling me that they have to figure out how to not only live under that roof, but work there as well? And actually get things done?" It was at that exact moment that I knew I had to get this book out there. In a quick, big way.

In an even bigger way, my community totally got behind me. And I mean my ENTIRE community, which is no small potatoes. It's huge, in fact,

So let's start with my truly amazing husband, Marty, who is, hands-down, my biggest cheerleader known to woman. Besides his unconditional love, which goes without saying, he is beyond supportive in everything I've done to change the lives of thousands of people around the world. Over 20 years, he's watched me grow, evolve, learn, fail, get back up, create, question, fail again, thrive, shine, pivot, and, and, and.... Through all of it, he's been my steady, my rock, and sometimes my guinea pig. So, the biggest thanks to you, Marty Ellin, for your unwavering everything. You keep me grounded, honest, and every time you tell me I'm a rockstar, I believe you. (Gosh, look how far I've come!)

To my daughters, Blair and Leah, nothing brings me more joy than to share with you how much I love what I do in the world, and how important it is to follow your bliss. You have been with me every step of the way since the day I came home from that crazy radio gig sobbing and said, "I'm done with this job." Who would have known that 20 years later, I would be building a platform to help change how the world works. Keep on embracing change, find the silver linings in everything, and keep doing what you love. Thank you for holding me up with more respect than I even asked for, and thank you for all your wise advice along the way. I love you both.

To my BIG FAM...thank you for cheering me on as I take my second dive into the author pool. I am so grateful to have every one of you not only in my corner, but more importantly as my tribe. To Matt, James, Drew, Jayne & Andy, Rachel & Jason, Richard & Marley, Steven & Karen, Lara & Jordan, Jaclyn, Lenny & Linda, Mickey & Ankita, Jeffrey & Heather, Justin & Gina, and Donna & George - we're a family with opinions, ideas, and stories . But regardless of whether we're always aligned, we are one. Backs and all. I love you and will always count on your support.

Krista Parkinson, if it weren't for you, I'm not sure this book would ʰppened. Certainly not when it did. When I told you that you need-
ᵉ the weekend to yourself to chill out, you answered, "I can't,

I'm going to the Bestseller in a Weekend 3-Day Intensive." Joining you in that experience was not the plan. At least, not until it was. Thank you, my friend, for sharing Alicia Dunams with me and for encouraging me to join you in one of the most intense, stressful, hysterically fun learning weekends ever. Watching your book *Get Hired in Hollywood* unfold before my very eyes revealed so much of the heart and soul of who you are. I am blessed with the gift of being the one who got to peer into your truly rich and interesting past so that you, too, can share your expertise and passion with the world. Through these books, both our journeys are paving the path for others seeking to travel in our lanes. You, my friend, are the real deal. Hollywood, and all those destined to get hired there, are lucky to have you front and center in their court.

Thank you, Alicia Dunams, for your weekend workshop jumpstart! Joining that class woke me up to a book I wasn't sure I had inside of me. It was the start of something I'm truly proud of.

Brian Johnson - you are the dude. Not only have you gotten me to the finish line in a time frame I never thought possible, but the pleasure of working with you has been nothing short of delightful. I knew from the moment we met that you would be instrumental in not only launching this book, but in helping me build a business that extends far beyond authorship. For that, and for the many gifts you've shared, (not to mention that killer smile), I am eternally grateful.

Kam and Peter, my dynamic duo. You guys are just what I needed to change my energy up around my business and how I was getting my message out into the world. You've pushed me out of my comfort zone, educated me to understand elements of this business I didn't care to know, and are a key driving force behind moving me forward. I am grateful for your brains, your availability, your collaboration with Brian regarding all things book related, and for reminding me that just being me is always my first job. And loving me nonetheless!

Tiffany & Matt Alley, you have not only been our "COVID pod" throughout these past 5 months, but you've been two of the greatest "new" blessings in my life. I have found myself saying as I age, "I don't need more friends, as I can hardly keep up with the ones I have." Meeting you later in life has added so much joy, laughter, self-reflection, and love to my already full bucket, I can't imagine my life without you in it. And while I'm well aware that it's Ruby (our golden doodle pup) who is at the heart of this relationship, you both have stolen mine as well. Thank you for sharing your home so graciously for me to write. I feel as much at-home there as I do mine. In fact, thank you for sharing all your homes with all three of us. Having St. Simons to go to for a short reprieve from quasi "lock-down" has been a Godsend, as have you, your encouragement, and your love.

Jennifer Jackson, wow! I could not have imagined what getting out of Atlanta and bunking down in your Granny's Cottage could have done for me, my energy, my focus, and my discipline. It was just what the writing doctor ordered! Offering your sweet space to me for 4 days to bring this book to completion was a gift of huge magnitude and changing up my environment did a world of good. Marty thanks you too, as I know he loved finally having the house to himself for a few days.

Thank you, Tish. You'll never know how much your guidance has meant to me. I've always considered you one of the finest, honest, raw, and engaging writers I know. So having you at a minute's notice to bounce ideas off of has carried me through my writing process. And no one supports what I do to help people live better, calmer, and simpler lives than you do. You are my star student, who got with my program right out of the gate. You have been living that way ever since, even when it meant throwing your stuff on the street praying someone would snatch it up in an hour.

Sussy, it is after you that Chapter 3: R.P.M. was named. You, my sweet "sister-from-another-mother," shared your wisdom of mindfulness meditation 7 years ago upon meeting. It has been the most important gift I have taken from knowing you. It's so important, that I continue to share you and your magic with my clients, my friends, and everyone who dares to sit in stillness, if only for 10 minutes. My 30-minute daily meditation has been life-changing. Almost as much as what our friendship has done to my soul since day one. I'd be lost without you, and even more lost without FaceTime.

To my Selden Beattie Rock Star team, you are far more than my "from-office-to-home" focus group. You have made me so proud to work with all of you over these years. Your stellar energy and attitude for your jobs really has proven that when you put your people first, your people deliver. There is not a slacker in the bunch. All are committed to learning, growing, adapting, and making sure you ask for what you need to be successful. Thank you, Beverly, for the opportunity to truly be a part of your team, and thank you for treating me as such. I'm grateful to solicit your teams' experiences so that everyone reading this knows they're not alone. There is solace, and power in knowing we are all in this together—a recurring motto of Selden Beattie for sure.

Shoshana Kreinces, my tush, thanks you ever so much for the Ergo Sit you gifted me as I had my last adjustment before heading on the road to my Writer's Hideaway! Whew...I don't want to even think about what this experience would have been like without it. It is a gift that will truly keep on giving.

To Marty, Tish, Sussy, Emily, Krista, Monica, Meg, Alan, Edward, Allyson, and Betty – thank you for allowing me to share your stories. It is from your real-life experiences that I am able to show others how it is possible to change the way you think, and the way you live, to get what you want out of your work, and your life.

To all those people who gave me your time to share your COVID-19 challenges, your frustrations, your work-at-home tools, and your silver linings...I could not have done this without you. As they say, "it takes a village." And it certainly does. I have a village of superheroes—way too many to mention—but you know who you are. You're smart, opinionated, honest, accomplished, encouraging, and willing to offer whatever I need to be successful. Thank you for your contribution to my cause.

To my social media community, thanks for letting me share this journey with you, and for letting me post questions to engage responses, not because I need to make Google happy, but because I honestly want your feedback. It's risky to put yourself out there when you're looking for feedback. Hell, it's just risky to put yourself out there, period! And while I can't please everyone, I honestly appreciate all your comments, likes, shares and support. And with the dramatically reduced face-to-face engagement happening these days, having social media as a way to connect is MY JAM. So glad it's yours too!

Thank you, everyone, for everything.

BOOK ENDORSEMENTS

I have known, and have been working with Wendy for more than two decades, and this work is her best yet. Wendy has captured a moment unlike any in our lifetime. And once again, she is showing us how to get s*&t done! Although there is nothing "new" about working from home, I don't believe that any of us could say that our current state seems "normal". In her work, Wendy has given us a route to sanity in what feels like insanity. Practical advice; humorous antidotes; and wise counsel abound in the pages of this book. This is indeed a must read for all of us who find ourselves in the pivot to what will become our future state.

Tim Phillips

General Counsel, American Cancer Society

Like most of us, I found myself suddenly working remotely with a full house and even fuller email inbox. The days stumbled in to each other with two teenage boys and a rescue dog underfoot. But a funny thing happened on the way to burn-out - life started finding order.

Without a commute, business and personal travel, sports practices, and obligatory social engagements, I started to slowly get around to what I hadn't made time to get around to...for years. I was sharing this with Wendy one day and she said, "Of course! We can finally get our actual house in order."

Our house, our schedule, our sleep, our email, our brains - it is possible. And this book is like having a personal coach on each page. Wendy offers a balance of the Why and the How. I found myself stopping several times to go take action and then come back and keep reading. I would sit with the ideas and then see how they unfolded in to action over the days ahead.

What Wendy offers is a simple, straightforward approach on how to step up your productivity. Get your life in order so you can get back to living (and loving) your life. Wendy will show you how.

Kristin Graham

Principal, Culture & Communications, Amazon

This entertaining, easy to read book will inform and inspire you to be as- or more- productive from home as you have been from your office. The stories and the creative tools Wendy shares are engaging and authentic, packed full of action steps that will help you navigate through the transitional to the new normal. Are you ready to get out from under your clutter and choose to live life in a different way? This book will launch that change!

Patrice Ciccarelli

Executive Development Program Manager/ Executive Coach

The Walt Disney Company

"This book is a gem! Wendy's high-energy conversational style zips the reader through dozens of user-friendly ideas for making our lives simpler, more enjoyable, and enormously more efficient and productive. There are ideas literally on every page that busy people will want to adopt. I desperately wish Wendy had written this book 30 years ago!"

Greg Riggs

Former General Counsel, Delta Airlines

"Wendy has always had such wisdom and sage advice in executive training and leadership development. With this new look at our world through the COVID lens, Wendy's approach is both timely and timeless. Her writing style is conversational and many of us have had similar questions, concerns, and fear about the "new working environment". Sit back, enjoy every word and as the pages fly by know that you are learning from one of the world's best known authors and scholars in how to work effectively and lead through a crisis."

Catherine Meloy

President/CEO, Goodwill of Greater Washington

" Wendy has taken a subject, (working from home), that we are just starting to grasp the magnitude of. In her book, she shares a powerful tool kit that anyone can start using immediately. The depth of her understanding comes from years of experience - this subject is not new to her and it shows. Her tools are practical and her wisdom and humor make it fun. Read her book and you will not only learn so many ways to be more productive at home, but you will also learn ways to enjoy your life more. As a past EVP of Human Resources, trying to understand and *support what was then a relatively small population of virtual employees, I really could have used Wendy. Now, her knowledge is essential for anyone trying to lead or support today's workforce. "*

Jill Ratliff

Principal, Jill Ratliff Executive Leadership, LLC

Table of Contents

BUT FIRST...BEFORE YOU BEGIN

So, you are about to go on a journey of sorts, with me. I'm going to roll out a toolbox for you to take what you need to organize all aspects of working from home, and beyond. And while I'm confident that everyone of these tools will help you increase efficiency, productivity, performance and peace of mind in your work, I never want to "put a round peg in a square hole." It's not my jam!

After reading and implementing these tools, if you feel like you want to dive more into how all of this can work for you, in a forum with others who share the same challenges as you, there's a way. It's called Work @ Home with Wendy 3-Day Intensive. A virtual event where we all gather to share, learn, work, create and restart our lives together. It's a game changer, for those that need more than just a book, but a community of like-minded, smart-working (instead of hard working) professionals ready to take their work-at-home experience to the next level.

Here's what some of the attendees have to say:

Honestly, I needed a good kick in the a** when it came to organizing my life. And, whoa did Wendy deliver! She's blunt, hilarious, no bs and just the kind of person I needed. When our 3-Day intensive class was over, I found myself emotional. The whole experience had been incredibly cathartic and I wasn't ready for it to end. I called her afterward and asked if we could figure out a way to keep her in my life for a while. I knew I needed the accountability to ensure I followed through. She was all in and willing to help me navigate putting her wealth of knowledge into practice. I am very, very grateful for all that I learned. While my legal practice will certainly reap the benefit of this experience, I have already seen how putting her words into action have improved my personal life and relationships. THANK YOU, WENDY! - Ashley

I was excited when I signed up for the 3-day virtual intensive with Wendy but as the time for class drew closer I was dreading giving up my entire weekend. HOWEVER, this was the best weekend I've had in a long time. I love the format of this program as it allowed me to put this system into action right away. I've been to many conferences and come home but never implement much of the things I learned. Since this was virtual from my own office, I was set up and raring to go Monday morning. Wendy is the most efficient person I've ever met; her no-nonsense, no-judgement, tell-it-like-it-is methods are so endearing you can't help but love her. I would recommend this to everyone; you won't regret it. - Elizabeth

Committing to this 3-day intensive was worth every minute for me. I started feeling "lighter" after day one and that feeling continued to evolve through day three. I'm excited to start my first week of "systems" which I know will work. Wendy's ability to explain how to modify our behavior to be more organized is amazing. Her systems are simple and anyone can do it. Her class is transformational! – Alyson

So, have a look at the book. Stay with it, start to finish. Be committed to implementing the tools, and if you find that you want, or need more, in the way of group or 1:1 support, reach out to me at wendy@wendyellin.com and let's chat. Or hop on to wendyellin.com and just flat out register for the next upcoming Work@Home with Wendy 3-Day Intensive - you'll be glad you did.

*The privilege of a lifetime is
being who you are.*

— JOSEPH CAMPBELL

1

My Story

"How the heck did you get into this crazy productivity consulting business?" is the most common question I get asked. It's not like they have a major for this in college, or any formal training that I'm aware of. Sometimes, the traits that come naturally wind up being the things we do best. And even if we do them well, we want to do them better, and the way we do them better is to practice, and boy, have I had practice. Have a seat, settle in, and I'll tell you more.

I was raised in a family of seven—two parents, and five kids all one year apart in age. We were a blended family, sort of like *The Brady Bunch*, only short one girl. My mom was twenty-eight years old when she became the mother of five, ages three, four, five, six, and seven. Yeah, I know, right? If I didn't live it, I couldn't imagine it either. But I did. And all things considered, we were somewhat normal in our family dysfunction. (Let's face it, doesn't every family have some level of it?) Seven humans in one small house, one bathroom shared by five. The basement was for the kids. We each had our own equal slice of a 10 foot cabinet for our toys. I always kept mine neat, so it was easy to find things. (And honestly, I'm not sure I had a choice.)

 While I'm not going to take you through the ins and outs of my childhood, what stands out the most for me were the rules. Wow, did we have them! Now, maybe if I were the parent of five kids, I'd have them too. (Actually, I did have them for my two, but not quite on the level of this.) There were rules regarding food, clothing, socializing, dating, bedtime, mealtime, weekends, thermostats, water usage, bathroom time, homework, television, bike riding, and just about anything you can think of. Oh, and let's not forget manners.

A somewhat typical afternoon looked like this: My sister and I shared a bedroom. We shared the closet, but we each had our own bed and dresser. That's pretty much all that fit in the room. At the end of the school day when we'd return home, we entered our room, only to find our entire dresser drawers dumped out onto the floor for us to re-fold and put back, because my mother was not satisfied with the way we were maintaining them. (For therapy, or another book, could she not have just asked us to do this over the upcoming weekend when our homework and dinner chores were not in the way?)

So that's a small glimpse into how I was raised (trust me when I say small). But to be honest, while the way some things were handled pi*ssed me off, the process of putting things back where they belonged in a way that made it easy to find things became MY JAM in every aspect of my life.

After college, I got into the advertising business. I started out on the agency side, as the traffic director of McCann-Erikson, back in the days of Tab. It was at that job that I discovered my ability to set up timelines, move projects forward, keep teams accountable and make deadlines work. I was organized while others had loose ends. I found that humor was a great way to get someone to do what I needed them to do to make something important happen.

Then after several years, I dipped my toe in advertising sales, where I sold, in succession, for a newspaper, art magazine, cable guide, and then radio time. That's when I really found my groove. I loved it, and I was good at it. Not because of brains, but because I had systems in place for getting things done. And when your income is based on 100% commission, you have to get things done. Sell, sell, sell, and then sell some more. So I did, and I did that efficiently and effectively for years, until the day came when I was done.

Enter the 25th Hour, Inc. A Personal Concierge company I purchased in 2000 from two Atlanta women each about to have their first child, literally within 10 days of one another. They were ready to close shop when a friend suggested I speak to them. Let's just say it was all in the timing. Two weeks later I owned a business. I remember waking up the next morning and saying to Marty, "Hon, I own a business. Now what do I do?."

I figured it out as I went, which I definitely would not advise, but at the time, what did I know? I had a few clients to serve, and I kept finding more. My sales muscle kicked in at just the right time. Yet my business how-to muscle was non-existent, and it required a serious, long-term workout.

For several years, I continued to run my very busy, wealthy and sometimes crazy clients lives for them, because they were too busy to run their own. Stuff like decorating Christmas trees, taking ladies to the hairdresser, taking older parents out to lunch, grocery shopping, dog walking, gift buying, wardrobe styling, office organizing, packing and unpacking homes—you name it, I did it. And honestly, it wore me down. I started to realize that the more I enabled these people to live this way, the longer they would. I started to feel bad for them and even worse for me.

That's when, in 2007, I flipped the model of my business. Instead of running your life for you, I was going to teach you how to live your life in a way that serves you well, so you never have to hire me again. And I've been going at it ever since.

Look, as I say, this is my JAM. I got this down. In my practice, and in this book, I'm sharing a tool box of what works for me and hundreds of others, to help you have the balance, productivity, and level of success you set out to achieve. I'm letting you inside the lives of those I've worked with who work from home to show you that you're not alone. Hardly. We are all challenged with things we aren't good at, things we're unfamiliar with, and even that which we are afraid of, and the pandemic has dumped a load of that on your plate, no? We're human. And the one thing for certain, during this COVID-19 experience, is that we're all in this together. Let your part of ordering your life into manageable pieces, sustaining your professional excellence while you manage healthy relationships, and reclaiming your sanity start with you.

The following chapters will include stories, ideas, systems, challenges, solutions and takeaways for all things relating to working-from-home: how to start your day, how to clean up your mess, how to get a hold of your paper, how to tame your technology, how to juggle your calendar, how to build in "me" time, how to get out of your own way, how to never be late again, and how to communicate in a world minus handshakes, hugs, and happy hour.

The change is in the choosing, my friend. If the way you're working from home isn't working for you, then read on. Choose whatever resonates with you, and put it into action. Your new work-from-home experience awaits you.

Oh, and one more thing. Thanks, Mom, for imposing your craziness on me. Because what came out of that has revealed my true calling, which I've loved sharing with the world ever since.

*Life is a journey. Time is a
river. The door is ajar.*

— JIM BUTCHER

2

Welcome Home, Marty. Or not!

It's March 16, 2020. I hear the car pull up outside my office window. Ruby starts barking because, she presumes, someone's here to give her love. Hopefully, it's Daddy. Yup, it's Daddy. Usually he saunters in, after doubling back to his car to get his wallet and phone, eager to let Ruby out to throw her the ball. This time, not so fast. He's literally unpacking his car of all the stuff he brought home from the office. We're talking laptop, briefcase, monitor, files, tech chords, mouse, desk chair, and who knows what else made its way into our home. Ok, now it's starting to sink in. He's coming home to work, like everyone else in the world. (Previously saying "world" felt like a slight exaggeration. Until now.)

The Atlanta mayor, along with all but 14 mayors in the country, declared a "shelter-at-home" policy starting immediately. And for us, it was 3/16/20. I'll never forget it.

I've had the luxury of working from home for 20 years. And yes, I call it a luxury. I have the house to myself, along with Ruby, my trusted companion. She makes sure I'm aware of anyone approaching the house, including the yard guys, the mosquito sprayer, the fitness trainer, and the squirrels teasing her outside the porch door. It's quiet when I need it to be. I set my own hours, go at my own pace, talk at my own voice level, break when I need to, and at this point, have this thing down pat. Not to mention that because I tend to walk my talk, I've set myself up to be uber-focused, productive and successful. I use the exact same systems, techniques, strategies and tools that I've shared in this book. Go figure.

Now here's what my new reality starts to look like: Marty starts out on the dining room table, where he's set up his laptop. He then takes the exact amount of books needed from my carefully curated bookshelf to lift his screen up so that it's the perfect height for a Zoom call. Then there's his Zoom calls. He can't figure out why he can't hear, hasn't done them enough (maybe ever) to know how to work it, and all I hear from the dining room is, "How do I get the sound to work? How do I let people into the room? How do I see all the boxes like *The Brady Bunch*?"

OMG, you're killin' me, dude! Take a freakin' Zoom lesson, for G--- sake! And Marty is not one to take a lesson until he's tried for at least an hour to figure it out by himself. Why save yourself time when you can waste an hour, only to get nowhere? And when I offer to help, he shoos me away. (He's a man.)

Next, he's decided the kitchen counter/island is a better place to work from, because the light is better. Only he's now inching closer to my office. And he's not pleased with the level at which I'm talking to my client, so he comes and closes my door. Which is fine, until Ruby decides she's had enough of my office and wants to get out. While I'm happy to let her out, I know it's not going to last long. It's minutes until she's decided she wants in again, at which point I'm getting up again to let her in. All while on a call with a client in the UK, who's 5 hours ahead of me and on the verge of bed time. Ridiculous, right? Oh, it keeps going.

Next, he's headed outside to our screened-in porch to test out taking a Zoom call there. Balancing his laptop on the huge candelabra out there, he settles in until the yard guys decide today is the day to mow the lawn, blow the leaves, and trim the hedges. Holy M of G! It's a s*it show of sorts over here in the Ellin house! And those yard noises, are they not the most intrusive, obnoxious sounds known to man?

That night we're having dinner, at which point I say, "Hey, hon, why don't we go online and order you a nice writing desk to put upstairs in that sitting area outside our bedroom? We never really sit there, you'll be far enough away from me so my voice won't be a problem, and you'll have your own space to yourself." His response: "I'm not sure it makes sense since I'll probably be going back to my office in a month anyway, so let's not spend the money." Famous last words!

So now it's May. The dates when the courts are going to open, which determines when Marty's office will "reopen," keep getting pushed back. So Marty's reopen dates do too. He's still moving from dining room to kitchen, to the porch, to the TV room and more often than not, upstairs in the sitting room. He's gotten really good at balancing his laptop on the candelabra up there too. And he's finally figured out, with a little tutoring from his colleagues, how to use Zoom, how to tune me out, and how to settle into this new normal that for now, and the foreseeable future, is what our work-from-home landscape looks like.

Finally, in July, he agreed to get the writing desk, and he loves having his own space to work where he only hears his Zoom call and not mine as well.

This, my friends, is our work-from-home scenario. I'm sure you're saying to yourself, "Whatever...I've got a husband, 3 kids, 2 dogs and a guinea pig. What are you complaining about?" And you know what, you're right. In the scheme of things, I've got very little to complain about. Yet now that we figured out how to make it work so that it works for both of us, no complaining necessary. We got where we need to be. We tested it out, moved it around, swapped it out for something else, tested it again, and eventually settled on the best arrangement possible for all parties involved.

Now it's your turn. My "home-team" is Marty and Ruby. Your "home-team" might include roommates, a mother-in-law, your kids and their kid, two cats and a goldfish. Whatever it is, meet with it. Talk to it. Recommend to it. Try things out with it. They're your people, and every member of your team deserves to be set up the best way possible to thrive (not merely survive) this coronavirus craziness, and all that goes with it.

Now let's get on with it, yes?

*Feelings come and go like clouds
in a windy sky.*

*Conscious breathing is my
anchor.*

— THICH NHAT HANH

3

R.P.M. (Rise. Pee. Meditate.)

The alarm goes off, you jump out of bed (ok, maybe not jump) and drag yourself to the shower, where your mind starts churning, and the autopilot begins. Stand in front of the closet, whine a little about having nothing to wear, grab the least offensive black pants, add a touch of gray on top, and off you go. Wait, off you go *after* you put your day face on, better known as makeup!

Kids, they're next. Wake them up, grab their clothes, then wake them up for real, and get them moving. Waffles in the toaster, coffee button on, lunches in the making. Check the time, check your email to see if any surprises await you at your office, holler at the kids to "move it," find the keys and head to the door.

OH, WAIT A MINUTE...NOT ANY MORE!

That's what some of our lives looked like pre-COVID. The routine that we could do with our eyes closed (and sometimes did!), right? But a routine, nonetheless. And that's exactly where I'm going with this.

With this new normal we keep referring to, the operative word here is NEW. What's the NEW way you're working now that you're home? What's the NEW way you are communicating with your "home team" now that you're all there together every day, all day long? What's the NEW way we're all socializing? (Physical distancing with masks.) What's the NEW way we're meeting with our staff/clients/families? (Zoom and FaceTime.) EVERYTHING IS NEW.

The definition of *new*: "not existing before; made, introduced, or discovered recently or now for the first time." While your old routine might have existed before to support your "going-to-the-office life," now is the time to discover your working-from-home routine. What if you got to start your day with a different sense of order, positive energy, and focus? What would that look and feel like for the rest of the day? **How you start your morning sets you up for the entire day, and it matters not what the routine is. It just matters that you have one.**

My dear friend Sussy (Anne Sussman, founder of Mindfulness Meeting Place) shared with me 7 years ago upon meeting that her morning routine started out with meditation. For most of her life, Sussy suffered from pervasive anxiety, always worrying about what-if's. "What if that happens, then this will happen, and OMG, what am I going to do then?" Down the rabbit hole of worry she went. It wasn't until she was 50 years old that she discovered meditation in a big way. She began to get quiet, sit in stillness, focus on her breathing, calm her mind, and change her brain. She started experiencing life differently than she ever knew was possible. It was from this awakening that she went on to become a certified meditation/mindfulness instructor, and she started her meditation coaching practice. (She's amazing. Google her now!)

I asked her to teach me how to meditate. Like perhaps you, I'm one of those who can't seem to ever turn off my mind. But even with an always buzzing brain, you can learn to sit in silence and focus on your breathing; the moment you notice you are in thought, bring your attention back to your breath. That, my friends, is what meditation is. Sussy says that when you stay on your thoughts, you're not meditating; you're daydreaming. And while there's nothing wrong with daydreaming, it's not meditating. Meditating is the practice of awareness, of being aware that your mind has wandered off your breath and onto what you're having for dinner that night, and when you notice that, bringing it back to your breath. Simple, right? Not so for many. But when you start meditating with intention, patience and self-love for 7 minutes a day, and increase to where I am at 30 minutes every morning, you will see a substantial difference in your attitude, your energy, your conversations, and most important, your stress levels. And to be honest, what this NEW working-from-home arrangement has revealed to so many of us is this: change is inevitable. It's unpredictable, it's alarming, it's scary, it's uncontrollable, it's confusing, it's unbelievable, it can be fatal, and it's happening to all of us. But responding to that change in a healthy way is not inevitable. Whatever anxiety you are experiencing just from the craziness that is known as 2020, starting out each day with some simple stillness can only be a good thing.

So, let's talk about establishing a routine. R.P.M. stands for rise, pee, meditate. It works for Deepak Chopra. What will work for you? I wake up every morning at about the same time, go to the bathroom, brush my teeth, splash some water on my face, and get right back in bed. I sit up against propped pillows and meditate for 30 minutes. Insight Timer is the app I use, and it works like magic. The chime sounds when I start, and it chimes again when I'm done. Sometimes I'm restless, impatient and ready to quit to get started with my day. But I don't. I sit there and take in all that this experience is there to give me. That's the first out of the six things I do every day as my morning routine. Wanna hear the rest?

1. **R.P.M.: Rise. Pee. Meditate.**

2. **Hydrate:** I start every morning with a cup of hot water with lemon. Wake my body up, get my metabolism going, then have my coffee. Then I continue to hydrate with water all day long. Your body needs this to regulate body temperature, to keep joints lubricated, to prevent infections, to deliver nutrients to cells, and to keep organs functioning properly. It also improves sleep quality, cognition, and mood. Damn, all that from little ole' H2O! So hydrate, people, hydrate!

3. **Move Your Body:** I like to get up and stretch before I even leave my bedroom. Or I'll do that while I'm getting dressed for the day. (Which these days is Lycra anyway, so I'm wearing stretch to stretch.) Then I'll go for a walk, workout with my trainer, or ride a bike. Exercising in the morning gives your body a healthy kind of fatigue and stress at the end of the day that results in deep and better sleep. Plus it ensures you actually do it, before your entire day gets away from you, before it's 9 pm, and there's no way you're doing it then. And...if taking a break in the middle of the work-at-home day to get away from your peeps works better for you, go for it. Just move your body!

4. **Express Gratitude:** I don't exactly remember when I started this, but it was at least 10 years ago, if not more. I have this lovely gratitude journal that sits on the corner of my desk right next to my computer. It's the first thing I touch when I sit down in my office. I write down the date, the words TODAY I AM GRATEFUL FOR...and I just write whatever comes to mind that morning. The sun shining into my office window, the amazing space I get to live in, the supportive family I have, the clients that I get to work with, the unconditional Ruby love, my women peeps that hold me up, the massage I'm about to get...Whatever I'm feeling, I write.

When you focus your energy on what you are grateful for (and Lord knows if nothing else, I am grateful not to have experienced this virus like so much of the world has), more things to be grateful for will show up for you. An attitude of gratitude is my JAM. Why not make it yours?!

5. Access Your Day: This is where in Chapter 7, I talk about huddling with your "home team." We have a work team that we connect with regularly on Zoom, and for some, way more than we'd like to. But what about our "home team"? They're the peeps who are right there in the everyday trenches with you, sharing the space, sharing the screens, sharing the toothpaste, and the home-schooling, and the meal prep, and the binge-watching, and the dog-walking, and, and, and. Your daily huddle with your "home team" is key to getting things done, staying on track, and maintaining some sanity. Then look at your work schedule to make sure you are set up to get your most important work done.

6. Get to Your M.I.T.s (Most Important Things) Every day brings new to-do's, new deadlines, and new challenges. And that was the case even when we went to an office to work. So regardless of where, when you're setting out to start your work day, focusing on what absolutely must get done today should be your first order of the day. This way, if nothing else gets done, you've at least gotten what had to be completed, not what you hoped to complete. Hard and fast deadlines, like "due to my boss by Thursday at 5" are non-negotiable. So make sure you get that done by Thursday at 5. But with other things on your plate that don't have those deadlines, you get to decide what gets done and what waits. Take it one day at a time. Prioritize based on need, not want.

That's my morning routine. It's a mindset. It's 99% non-negotiable. It's doable. It's empowering. It's beneficial. It's comforting, and it's mine. Now go create your own.

WORK FROM HOME NOTES

WORK FROM HOME NOTES

WORK FROM HOME NOTES

WORK FROM HOME NOTES

*The way you do anything is the
way you do everything.*

— TOM WAITS

4

Your Success Is Under Your Mess!

It's April 2013, and an old friend of mine calls to ask me a favor. My curiosity has me intrigued as she proceeds to share, "My sister in California really needs you. She's maxed out on everything: stress, time, email, clutter, and fatigue. She can't focus, doesn't sleep, and on and on she went. First thing that came to mind, "I wonder if her sister even thinks she *needs* help." But after learning that the sister "might finally *be there*," I agreed to talk to her. So we get on the phone, and as anticipated, she spills out her current reality to me, without so much as taking a breath between sentences, as if she just finished the Boston Marathon. Holy mother of God! Like a bat out of hell, she downloads me on all that's not working in her big ole successful, Hollywood producer life, and her take actually mirrors exactly how her sister described it, just the day before. And before you know it, I'm on a plane to LA to move in with her for a week to help her (hopefully) transform her life.

Let the games begin! After waiting two hours in LAX for her to get me (she was running late), I was finally on my way to witness, first-hand, the life and times of Tish. The second we completed the home tour of her adorable 900 sq. ft. Hollywood craftsman-style house, she was out the door. Off to work the 1-11pm shift, managing her production team at the Warner Brothers Studios, which she had hoped would be her dream job when she moved her whole life across the country at age 50. The job didn't quite turn out as planned, but it had gotten one of her kids through college debt-free, and it allowed her to live the lifestyle to which she was accustomed. Tish was already dreaming about taking a leap of faith and starting over (again), but that meant first getting her s*it together. Because sometimes you can't see, or even think clearly, when there's so much stuff in the way.

The word *clutter* actually comes from the word *clotter*, to clot. So just like a blood clot prevents blood from flowing freely through your body, any kind of clutter (physical, emotional, spiritual) can keep you from navigating your life with ease, and it can hinder (or even extinguish) the decision-making process.

Enter Wendy Ellin. As it turns out, as quickly as Tish spoke, that's how quickly I work. Reminiscent of the White Tornado, right out of the gate, I literally "gutted" every surface, cabinet, drawer, and bookshelf. Anything that could hold something got cleared. Right onto the floor. And it was from there that the magic began.

Clutter is nothing more than the manifestation of indecision. So you don't decide about this, and you don't decide about that, etc., etc., etc., and before you know it, your entire life is in piles that grow, become an obstacle, and gather dust awaiting a decision that's never coming.

You're probably asking yourself, "What does this have to do with working from home?" Ok, so here's the answer. Your work-from-home life cannot just be carved out of what is left from the rest of your life. Your W-F-H space cannot just be an afterthought...it has to be carefully considered and tailored to meet the special needs of your job, while considering the circumstances of your home. Keep reading, because it *is* possible to get there, no matter where you are right now!

Take a look around you. What do you see? For many, it is miscellaneous stuff spread out across your dining room table, in the guest room, on the steps, and in other places that are so cluttered, you and your family have to literally watch every step. Tish was by no means a hoarder, but her sh*t was in the way of her productivity, and if you're like her, or most people that I've recently interviewed about working from home, you and your family have unconsciously compromised the pleasure of your living areas as the common challenges and distractions of your daily life (aka crap) start to creep in, one by one, with you barely noticing.

As you have experienced, how you live in your everyday life doesn't just go away because you're now working from home. And if the new "normal" is challenging your sanity, your relationships and your success at work, it's time to change that! Unless of course you're uber productive, enjoying this W-F-H experience, and all your cylinders are cranking full force. But I'm thinking if you're reading this book, that ain't happening.

Back to the clutter. Does your work computer share the dining room table with the family's 1000-piece puzzle? Do you have a garage that your car can't fit into because of the bicycles, lawn mower, hockey sticks, garden tools and baby stroller? (Your kids are teenagers; dump it already!) What about your kitchen drawers? Have you designated one full drawer as your "electrical bin" where miscellaneous cords and plugs take residence? Do you actually still own the equipment that goes with those cords?.

So many people live above their means "spatially." Read that again.

That means you have more stuff than your actual house can effectively hold!

Here's my theory about this: I'm sixty-three years old (I know, right?), and like everyone else, I've been collecting stuff throughout my entire life. Six decades worth of stuff—you can imagine how much that is! I'm a pretty healthy woman. I eat carefully, exercise regularly, and do what it takes to keep my mental health intact. So given this, I may have the chance to live at least another 20+ years. Therefore, if I don't get rid of some of what I've collected over the past sixty-three years, where the hell am I putting what's coming in over the next twenty? Oh sure, I can certainly rent a storage unit to house the things that can't fit in my house. "How's that working for you?" I ask you once again! Why pay to house stuff that didn't even make the cut to stay in your home to begin with? I say toss it, save the money, and use the extra dollars to help set up your new at-home work space.

Back to Tish in LA. It's not what her home looked like that had her in full-blown overwhelm; it's the way her home functioned that wore her down. If the clutter and disarray doesn't affect how you live, then continue to live that way. I only focus on what doesn't work, because "if it isn't broken, don't fix it." But for Tish, she was ready to leap out of a 30-year career into the unknown, and was so stuck in her everyday routine, so worn down by the lack of clear space to think, that there was no energy left for creating what she truly wanted. Her crazy-ass job was HER priority, because it had to be. I remember this like it was yesterday. We're at the Urth Cafe on Melrose Ave. It's Sunday morning at 9 am, and we've just placed our breakfast order. While waiting outside to hold our table, Tish gets a text that a well-known actor just lost his life due to suicide. Yes, really. So Hollywood, right? In that instant, we get up, grab our food to go, and together, we sprint to her office where she starts pulling clips to compile the story to be thrown together quickly to make air. It was that day, that experience, that truly reminded Tish what was most important to her: she was finally ready for her life to be her own. And while she needed to live her priorities, she couldn't get traction on changing that because she was weighed down by clutter in every part of her life, especially her home. So the next morning, we got real serious about setting up her home so that she could focus on *her* life, not everybody else's. It was time to clear the path for her to ditch this soul-crushing, all-consuming job in order to create her dream—a transformational playground for women all over the world to come together, discover their passion, and take a quantum leap forward, just like Tish did, once she got out of her own way. (And by the way, Campowerment has been thriving now for 7 years, and evolving every day. You definitely want to check it out at campowerment.com.)

CLEARING THE PATH

Ready to clear your path? Okay, here's my 3 Box Process for De-cluttering every space in your home. Yes, I said *every* space. Please don't do this halfway. Go all in. I swear you'll thank me for this, and your work-at-home, and live-in-your-home experience will completely transform.

Box 1: This is for trash. Get a box, a plastic garbage bag, a dumpster, I don't care. You're going to choose one space to start—whatever room stresses you out the most. For Tish, her home was small enough that we just dumped everything in the home on the ground, tossed what we could (see below), then put back what she was keeping in the place that made the most sense to her and to how she lived. So first, you're just making decisions about what stays and what goes. Try to make quick decisions, and use the "less is more" mentality when doing this, or you won't make much headway in the tossing column. Remember what the ultimate goal is: to have less stuff than you started this project with.

Box 2: This is the stuff you don't want, but maybe someone else you know does. It could be a file that you brought home from the office to use but don't need anymore. But your colleague might. It could be a photo frame that you don't even like, but your daughter might want. Anything you find that you know you don't need to keep, but might serve someone else or make them happy, goes in Box 2.

Box 3: These are the keepers. Let's talk about the criteria for what stays. I only want you to keep what you NEED and what you LOVE. THIS IS

REALLY IMPORTANT. There's an important word missing here. (It's not WANT.) The word that is missing, that I want you to get out of your vocabulary when it comes to this process, is LIKE. Get that word out of the equation. Because after all, WE LIKE EVERYTHING. That's what gets us into this mess to begin with. We see it, we like it, we buy it. But we don't love it; we just like it. And up until now, that's been a good enough reason to take it home with us. Until now. But going forward, no more buying because you like it. Only buy it because you LOVE it. If you have in your life, in your closet, on your shelves, and in your home only things that you LOVE, your life will change dramatically for the better. You will find joy in sitting on your sofa and seeing the things you love. You will go in your closet every day and only choose from the clothes you LOVE. Because that's all you'll have to choose from. Your home is meant to create joy, not jobs.

While we're on that subject, let's talk about black pants. (Sorry guys, this is for the ladies.) Do you regularly find yourself in your closet sliding all those black pants aside to find the ones that fit? The only ones you wear these days because they make you feel better than all the others? So why, may I ask, do you even have the others? Why not get rid of the ones that no longer fit? They're just reminding you that they don't fit, which then reminds you that your body isn't what it used to be, which then takes you down that God-forsaken rabbit hole of beating yourself up for letting your body go. Or whatever your story is, because Lord, we certainly all have one. Get those blessed size 4s and 6s and whatever is no longer your size out of this closet RIGHT NOW. And then listen to me because I'm going to share what might be the most important 8 words you'll read in this chapter. Ready?

"THEY'RE NEVER GOING TO STOP SELLING BLACK PANTS."

Until the day the entire universe takes its last breath, there will be a store that sells black pants. Ditch every pair that doesn't fit, or that doesn't make you feel like the rock star goddess that you are, and watch what happens. You will actually like getting dressed in the morning. There will be no negative reminders or past-size haunts, just choices that make you feel good. Now that's what I call closet confidence.!

While we're on the subject of closets—ladies, when it comes to shoes, try adopting the policy that if you bring a pair in, a pair goes out. Look, we only have two feet. And these days, where are we going? I don't know about you, but my butt hasn't seen a pair of pants since March. My go-to outfit is Lycra. Yup, every day I'm in exercise leggings and a tank top. And if I have a Zoom meeting, I make sure to change the top to look as professional as I can, so shoes can mostly be an afterthought. But I do realize that there are those of you who feel better getting dressed "for work" in the morning before reporting to your laptop. Go for it. It's just not my jam, so I'm choosing Lycra. You gotta do what works for you. But when it comes to shoes, only have what you need and LOVE...and doesn't bring you pain.

Tish has adopted this shoe thing and says it's working fabulously. She's committed to getting rid of what she doesn't wear, clearing room for something new. And again, if the shoe no longer fits, or those 3 ½ inch stilettos only make it to the car before your feet are killing you, isn't it time to say goodbye? Why do we have to get older to realize that comfort is key? I'm not willing to risk being in pain for fabulous calves. I'm just not. But if you are, have at it.

Okay, so there's your process. Three boxes: toss, give away, and keep. Keepers must be what you need and love. Toss box needs to go in your car to be dropped off as soon as possible so you're not tempted to take things back out. Keepers now need a permanent home. That's right, if you're keeping it, it must have a place to live. *And a pile is not an option.* An option is a shelf, a bin, a wall, a drawer, a cabinet, a bookshelf, a file cabinet, a chest, and anything that you can put something onto or inside of. Not a random common area horizontal surface that's just waiting for you to clutter up. Don't do it.

Resist the temptation and give everything the permanent home it deserves. And you deserve even more.

Once you've completed the decluttering, you can now focus on finding the perfect place to set up your "W-F-H" space. So let's get creative. If you have a guest bedroom, that might make the most sense since visitors might be few and far between these days, and you will have a door to close. If not, can you get an inexpensive writing desk to put in your bedroom? Maybe tuck it in a corner by rearranging some furniture. The key is to create a space that will keep you away from the center of your home. One that will give you the most privacy possible. One you can settle into for the work day. One that promotes productivity and focus, not stress, chaos, and dysfunction.

- ► When creating that space we're talking about, here's a list of things to consider:

- ► The lighting—natural is always the best

- ► Accessible outlets necessary for technology, lamps, etc.

- ► Your chair—comfortable and adjustable is key

- ► Desktop space for only necessities

- ► Small whiteboard for daily task reminders

- ► The least amount of distractions as possible

We'll talk later about more tools you might need to ensure remote work success. For now, let's find your best work-from-home space. You deserve it. So get creative. Think out of the box.

One more thing, speaking of boxes. After this process, I suggest you place a large empty box on the floor somewhere in the center of your home. Write on the side of the box "USE IT OR LOSE IT." Every time you come across something that you realize you don't use, need or LOVE, toss it in the box. Have everyone in your home play this game with you. See how much you can collect to be given away at the end of the month. You'll be amazed, when you start looking for things, how much shows up. Go for it.

So what happened to Tish? Well, let me wrap up our journey together for you. I stayed for the entire week, we tossed OUT 27 plastic garbage bags full of stuff, took 3 car loads to Goodwill, and she's been loving life ever since. Her cadence has slowed down, and she's a happier camper now. Was it tough? Sure it was. Making decisions with things isn't always easy. It's probably why you haven't done it until now. She had this broken mirror leaning against the dining room wall hidden behind a chair. "What's this?" I ask. Tish says, "Oh, it's a mirror that fell in the last earthquake and broke. "OMG, you're killin' me, girl," was all I could say. She was holding onto a broken mirror! If that's not bad ju-ju, I don't know what is! I took the mirror, walked it out to the curb, and invited her to say goodbye. Tootles, it was gone in an hour.

Two bad-ass total strangers came together for a week. And what came from it turned out to be a life transformation for both, and a friendship with one of the most hilarious, raw, evolving, soulful women I know. With her path cleared, Tish powered forward. She is now 7 years into Campowerment, her new job (I mean joy). After "sheltering-at-home" in FL with her 91-year-old dad for the past 5 months, she's picked up her life once again and moved to Philadelphia. Yup, changing it up, and here's the coolest thing about that. She hasn't been able to fly back to LA since the lock down, but she has a house full of belongings that need to be packed and shipped to PA. But since she's been maintaining (and loving) her organized home, she FaceTimes the people renting from her, walks them through the house, has them pack what she wants, dump or donate what she doesn't want, and never has to go back to that house again. Can you imagine what that process would be like if it was the "before Wendy house"? I'm just sayin' having an organized home is a gift that keeps on giving.

WRITE THIS DOWN:

1. Declutter each space with the 3 Box Process.

2. Set up "USE IT OR LOSE IT" box in your home

3. Keepers must have a permanent home.

4. Sniff out the best place for you to set up your work space.

WORK FROM HOME NOTES

WORK FROM HOME NOTES

WORK FROM HOME NOTES

WORK FROM HOME NOTES

When patterns are broken, new worlds emerge.

— TULI KUPFERBERY

5

The Pitfalls of Paper

Most of the people I work with straddle both the paper and technology worlds. We all communicate and perform moving back and forth between the two. Let's face it, until the mailman stops delivering mail to our homes, we can't consider our world paperless. And I'm thinking that's not going to happen any time soon. So, if you toggle between both worlds, you need to have a system for both. First, let's focus on paper.

Picture this. Emily runs a successful PR agency out of her home office. She employs and manages 3 others working remotely, while juggling the demands of 40+ clients nationwide pretty much seven days a week. Emily is balancing technology (and finance, personnel and other balls) reasonably well, but the paper that goes along with sustaining this business is out of control. That's Emily's reality. And it's doing a number on her energy and sapping her ability to find things when she needs them. It's especially discouraging, when her clients need them. She spends way more time *looking* than *doing*. Sound all too familiar?

I met with Emily to see what she was stressed out about, and sure enough, it didn't even start with work issues. (It almost never does; it's about how you live your everyday life first. Work is just where you suffer from it most.) As it happens, her dad passed away a year before, and she couldn't find a way to start filtering through the paperwork.

Paper will creep in with little to no effort on our part. But unfortunately, it won't leave without some effort. So we got to work. And just as Tish had important threshold decisions to make about whether things stayed or went, so did Emily with her paper. When too much paper is clogging up your life, ask this first: "Where did it come from?" Sure, it comes from the mail that the mailman delivers to our mailbox, and there's stuff you brought home from the office at the beginning of this "lockdown." However, most times, it comes from your computer. You printed it. I'd say 95% of the paper in our lives exists because we printed it from our own computer. Stop that! Only print what you need (do you really need it? See below before reflexively saying yes). Or if you do print it, toss it when you're done. But...if you need to keep it, it needs a permanent home. (Sound familiar?) And in this case, that would be a file cabinet. Because remember, a pile is not an option. For all the paper that has come into your life but has not left, no matter the source, I'm going to share the system that I taught Emily, that everyone reading this can implement anywhere. Yup, even in your W-F-H office.

Before sharing the system, this is really important. Everything that comes into our life falls into one of three categories. If it's not TRASH, it's either a TO DO or a TO SAVE. That's it. There are only three places to put things: the TRASH, the TO DO place and the TO SAVE place.

THE SYSTEM

Now for the system. This system has actually been around for decades and is shared and spoken about by many in the field of professional organizing. I call it my *COMMAND CENTRAL*. It's how Emily and I maintain our lives, and we now both use it throughout each day. In its simplest form, it is referred to as the age-old "tickler system." We are going to start making decisions with everything that comes into our life—**WHEN IT COMES IN!** And having this system is a key to helping make that happen.

To clarify, this chapter is focusing on the things that come into our life in **PAPER** form. There are other things that come our way like emails, voicemails, requests from others, and things that randomly pop into our head. Emails have their own chapter, so not to worry. (Aren't they special!) The other items we just capture with paper and then put into the COMMAND CENTRAL as well. For example, you're on a Zoom call and your boss asks you to do something. Jot it down on a card, and pop that card in your TO DO system. You get a follow up email with the TO DO's you're responsible for? Print it out and put it in your system. Walking for exercise and suddenly you remember you forgot to call the vet back? Jot it down when you get home and pop it in your system.

So now, the processing part! What if I told you that from this day forward, you were going to start processing everything that comes into your life (regardless of how it arrives) *as it arrives*? Don't freak out; it's much easier than you think. You see, one of the main problems with clutter is that things come into our lives in one of the five ways noted above, but since we have not created a processing system or a place for them to go, they don't go anywhere and ultimately form the piles you currently have on the kitchen counter, on your bedroom floor or elsewhere. So our goal is to create a place for what we are keeping so that we only have to put our hands on it when we need it next.

If you are willing to let it, this Command Central System WILL CHANGE YOUR LIFE! Here's what you will need:

▶ A file box/bin or desk/file cabinet drawer to house this system

▶ Three boxes of 25 hanging folders (either letter or legal size, depending on the size of your file drawers). Yes, that's right—those army green (not so attractive) hanging files we all use in offices around the world. (But wait, they now sell them in colors, so go for it!)

- ► 3x5 cards

- ► Colored dot stickers

Now you are ready to start setting it up.

The system requires:

- ► 31 hanging files with tabs numbered 1-31 on them

- ► 12 hanging files with tabs labeled January through December

- ► 3 "special" files outlined below

- ► 25 hanging files left over to use when setting up your reference documents (TO SAVE) that you file alphabetically

- ► The colored stickers to represent weekends in your system

The basics are the 31 days of the month, the 12 months of the year, and the alphabetical reference folders. *DOES IT GET ANY SIMPLER THAN THE DAYS OF THE MONTH, THE MONTHS OF THE YEAR, AND THE ABCs?*

Each folder's tab should have a number on it (1-31) or a month of the year (January-December). That would amount to forty-three hanging folders plus the three "special" files I will share with you, totaling forty-six hanging folders in your Command Central drawer or file box. The remaining box of twenty-five folders should be set aside to create your alphabetical TO SAVE reference files for those documents you want to keep for future use.

Place the dot sticker on the days that represent the weekends in the current month. That is the only thing that changes month to month in the set-up of the system, besides the stuff that you put in the folders.

3 Special Files:

Special File #1: **READY REFERENCE.** This is the very first file in your drawer before the number 1 file. It is where all the things live that you most frequently put your hands on and refer to. I have my passwords in that file so I don't have to look them up every time I can't remember one, which is often. I also put some "cheat" sheets I often use, like how to use FreeConferenceCall.com or Zoom Basics. It's great for phone numbers you often use, like those for your team members you need to access since working remotely. I keep things that most people post on their corkboard in front of them (which is just another form of distraction to me) in this file. I don't want all that stuff in sight, but I still want it near me for easy access.

Special File #2: **AWAITING RESPONSE.** This is a great file for housing all those things that you are waiting for from someone else—instead of them living in a pile on your desk or in a "metal clutter holder," they are in a file that is right behind Ready Reference. I look at that file almost every day to see what is outstanding in the event it's been a few days and I may want to remind someone that I am waiting for their response. Again, this is a great file to have.

Special File#3: **RIP & READ.** This file ROCKS! You know all those magazines you have piling up against the wall in your bedroom/bathroom—high enough that they could serve as an end table—because you don't have time to look through, much less read them? Now, every time you get a magazine, give yourself twenty-four hours to go through them and rip out the articles you want to read, staple the corner, and pop them in your RIP & READ file for when you have time to read them. Then discard the magazine itself. Take the Rip & Read file with you to your next medical appointment. I never mind having to wait at a doctor's office because I look at it as built-in time to read from my R&R file—wouldn't you rather read something of your own choosing than some 2005 *Motor Trends* magazine with half the pages missing? Try that the next time you go to the doc's office—you'll be amazed at how less stressed you are about waiting!

Okay, so now that we have set up all the critical files that comprise your Command Central, you are ready to start processing what remains from the *PURGING* session I spoke of in Chapter 4. We are now going to give our attention to the box/basket into which you put all the things you really must keep and tackle—are you ready...? One piece of paper at a time!!

COMMAND CENTRAL

COMMAND CENTRAL

FIVE STEPS FOR PROCESSING:

Remember, everything that comes into our lives falls into one of three categories. It's either something we need to take action on (TO DO), it's something we may want to refer to sometime in the future (TO SAVE), or it's something that can be thrown away (TRASH). So we start by taking one of five steps to determine what happens with every single thing that comes your way.

1. *LET IT GO* – This is where you get rid of what you don't need or love. Plain and simple...once you get the hang of it! So when something comes into your life, the first thing you are going to ask yourself is, "Do I need to keep this?" As I've said before, I'm not suggesting you toss anything you truly need to keep. I want you to start strengthening that "LETTING GO" muscle so that you are only left with what you love or need to keep. Make this your first threshold decision: *do I really need to retain this?* Trust me, once you get good at "letting go," you will be amazed at how good it feels.

Assuming you do not throw it away, choose from the following four steps:

2. **LET IT GO TO SOMEONE ELSE:** For those of you who have others to delegate to, rejoice in this option and set these items aside to put in your system after your sorting and discarding are done!

A note about delegating: For a long time, I had no one to delegate any of my work to, so this choice was not an option for me, and it may not be one for you. But if it is, start honing in on your delegating skills so you can empower those who work with you and leave what is unquestionably your work to yourself. The key to effective delegating lies in one word: communication. Are you asking for what you need, and are you in agreement as to when you will receive it? I am a firm believer that there can never be too much communication when it comes to asking someone to do something for you, and how you ask is as important as the task at hand. Know what you hope to accomplish and state that expectation in clear terms. Confirm that the delegatee knows what is expected of her/him, and the time frame for completion. The conversation between you and the delegatee should enhance your effectiveness, accomplish the necessary task, and promote real cooperation between you.

3. *DO IT NOW:* This is a great one! It's for all those things that come into your life that you can respond to in **TWO MINUTES OR LESS!** That's right, make it happen and get it off your plate. Most two-minutes-or-less things actually take less than that.

A note about doing it now: We will talk about this more in Chapter 4 when we tackle our email inbox. But for now, it's important to see this step as one that will quickly eliminate much of what is waiting for you to handle. Once it is handled, you will feel like you just completed the "quick weight loss" plan. It requires a trained eye and some serious focus to get in, respond in two minutes or less and move on, but this is a discipline well worth developing. This is actually my favorite processing step—it allows me to get in, get out, and get rid of. So for all those messages that you can return, all those emails you can respond to, all those requests you can process in two MINUTES OR LESS, as NIKE so aptly puts it...JUST DO IT! That means taking a break at intervals during your day to see how many of these you can get out of your inbox or out of your voicemail box.

4. *File in (TO DO) FURTHER ACTION files* – These are the files in your COMMAND CENTRAL. It's where all the items you need to take further action on go until you need to see them next.

A note on COMMAND CENTRAL FILES: At the point you begin sorting items into your Command Central TO DO files, you'll need to decide whether you need each individual item during one of the days left in the current month (1-31) or in a future month (January – December).

For example, let's say you have a Zoom meeting next week on August 20th. It's a new client and you want to be prepared. So you print out some docs to read up on them before the meeting. Put them in the "19" file in your Command Central. This way when Aug. 19th rolls around, and you see on your calendar that your meeting is the next day, you will have the stuff you want to read in preparation waiting for you in today's file. It sure beats having to scramble that morning to find the reading material then. Print it and file it when it's top of mind, and it will be there waiting for you when you need it. This system not only keeps you organized and on top of what you have going on in your world, it saves you loads of time in having to look for things that are important to your success.

IMPORTANT DISTINCTION HERE: Distinguish between "where you go" and "what you do" on a daily basis. That means don't have your "to go's" and your "to do's" in the same place. My "to go's" go on my calendar because they relate to a specific time (i.e., lunch appointment, client meeting, Zoom call, doctor appointment, etc.). My "to do's" go in my Command Central in the day that I want to get started on a certain project, or when it is due, depending on how long it takes to complete. I put my appointments on my calendar and then anything, like directions to that appointment, go in my CC on the day of the appointment.

Another example...you make flight reservations for a trip you are taking in November, and it's July. (Yes folks, I am counting on traveling coming back sometime soon!) Print out the electronic ticket and put that in your November file. You'll never need to search for it on your computer or wonder where that information is because as long as you remember that the trip is in November, you'll be able to find it. Or better yet, create a file folder with the name of the trip on the tab (i.e., Portugal/2021 - a girl can dream, can't she?), and everything including travel details goes in this folder and the folder lives in November. Then when it's November, take it and put it into the daily file for the day you are leaving. Make sense?

ʒcem allows you to plan ahead, so do just that. If you have a hard ɪast deadline of next Friday, and the project takes a day or two to do, put those documents in the Wednesday before the deadline to give yourself the time you need to complete it. Always build in time for "unexpected interruptions"—the best way to handle them is to EXPECT THEM!

For those of you who would rather remain more electronic when it comes to processing your life, stay tuned. We will delve into that in *Chapter 6, Declutter Your E-clutter*!

5.   *File in (TO SAVE) FUTURE REFERENCE file* – This is where all the things that you need to keep that are not action items live. Whether you need to refer to something once a year or once a week, it must have a permanent home in a reference file. Otherwise, it will be living in a pile instead of a file, and that will only bring you right back to where you started, so let's not go there. I have a "Personal To Save" file drawer and a "Business To Save" file drawer. Each has their own set of hanging file folders. My Personal File Drawer has folders that say Apple, Bicycles, Delta, Edward Jones, Household, Instruction Manuals, Ruby, Warranties, etc. All the necessary documents that I need to keep live in a file in this drawer. I name the file what the document is (Automobile Info) and file it alphabetically. So if my husband is looking for anything, it will be in our Personal TO SAVE drawer filed alphabetically. The same goes for my Business TO SAVE drawer. There are files for clients, marketing, social media, website, and then sub-folders for topics I collect information on such as clutter, self-defeating behaviors, technology, etc. The easiest way to name a file is to call the file what you would call the document category. The first name that comes to mind is usually what you would look for, so try calling it that. This doesn't need to be difficult; it needs to be simple and make sense to you.

So there you have it—the five steps you have for processing everything that comes into your life. When you complete this process of setting up your Command Central and touching everything to determine where it goes, you will end up with:

1. Only what you need or love remaining because you've tossed the rest.

2. Items that you either 1) will delegate and are now tucked in your Command Central or 2) that you already delegated to others and are in a follow-up system for tracking them. (Remember to take an "Action Card," write the task you delegated and place in your system on the day before it's due to remind yourself that you are expecting it the next day. See the section below on Action Cards.)

3. A bunch of "to do's" that either took two minutes or less to respond to so you did—and they are no longer on your plate—or that are in your Command Central waiting to be done when you get back to your work at hand.

4. All your TO DO items that you have put in your daily or monthly files so that when the time comes, you will be reminded to do them.

5. A home for all non-action TO SAVE items for you to access when you want to—or how about this: your partner can access them because you now have an easy A-Z file to work from.

6. Once you take the time to get yourself "up to date"—meaning you have tackled the piles everywhere and there is nothing else to process from your past build-up—all you have to do is process it day by day. And when you get in the habit of making quick decisions with everything, probably in about twenty-one days, you will be amazed at not only how good you get at it, but how freeing it feels to touch it, move it, and forget about it.

Now you are really turning your head off when you turn the lights off at night! Congratulations! You've earned it!

5 CHOICES POSTER

Make 1 of 5 choices

Let it go

Let it go to someone else

Do it now

Further action file

Future reference file

W E N D Y   E L L I N
Workplace Productivity Strategist
Productivity • Performance • Peace of Mind

Prioritizing Made Easy

Now that you have essentially taken your "to do's" and put them in your system, all you have to do is prioritize your day, and if you really want to, you can get rid of your to-do list! Here's why I hate to-do lists. You have this long laundry list (on what I refer to as an "*illegal* pad"—I hate those things) of all the things you have to do in your life. Some are personal, some are professional, but it's all-inclusive. Some need to be done this week, some need to be done next month. But so you don't forget about them, they remain on your list. Then as you complete something, you cross it out. Now you can hardly distinguish the remaining outstanding "to do's" from the ones you've crossed out—so you flip the page and start another list. The list never ends, and you never stop writing one. Ugh—what a mess of a system! All a list does is remind you of what you have to do, but it doesn't indicate when you have to do it. Sure, I have a ton of stuff to do, but why would I want to carry around a list to stress me out about how much I have to do?

This is where those **3x5 "Action" Cards** come into play. Instead of putting all your to-do's on a list, put them on cards, one item per card. This way, you can take that card and place it in the day or month in your Command Central for when you plan on doing it. Drop it in your Command Central and forget about it! You'll get to that day when it arrives, and your to-do will be waiting for you.

I have 3x5 cards with my logo and company information. I carry them with me when I go to a meeting. When someone in the meeting asks me to do something for them (get them an email address or phone number, put together a proposal, etc.), I pull out a card and write the to-do on the card and when I get back to my office, I pop the card in my CC. I also give people information they may need from me on a card as well—it's another way of marketing your name and business out there in front of the world. People always ask me about my cards, which means they take notice!

With the Command Central, we have essentially turned your TO DO list into a TO DO system—a place where you only see/touch it when you need it next instead of seeing the same thing on your list for weeks unending. It's a challenge for those of you who treat your TO DO list as if it were your Bible. I get it. But once you adapt this new habit and see how it feels to stop listing your day and start planning your day, you'll never want to make a list again. Now all you have to do is prioritize each day as it arrives and allow this system to offer the flexibility our lives ask of us. If you can't get to it today because something else became a bigger priority (and in most cases, plan for that to happen), move it to tomorrow and do it then. This system is not meant to be carved in stone. If you let it, it will be a flexible, adaptable, and simple solution to getting control of your workload and your life once and for all. Your TO DO list will become a "TA DONE" list. (Thank you, Tim Phillips!)

And oh, back to Emily. She's killing it in her office. She swears by her COMMAND CENTRAL, and literally reaches out to me every March reminding me of her joy due to not having to change her colored dot stickers representing the weekend because February and March weekends always fall on the same days. It's the small things, folks, that can bring such joy! She's got total control over her workload, takes each day as it comes, doesn't stress out over the big picture, expects change, and focuses more on making her clients successful now that the way she works actually works for her.

WRITE THIS DOWN:

1. **Order supplies for COMMAND CENTRAL**

2. **Go through paper purging process.**

3. **Set up CC and Reference File**

4. **Load up your system**

5. **Go, baby, go!**

6. The only thing you should have on your desk every day is the daily folder for that day and the contents in it. Start working on the highest priority item and conclude with the lowest priority item. Be confident enough to know what needs to be done when and if you need to move projects/tasks around to accommodate your ever-changing life, and do it with ease and assurance that tomorrow is another day—and it will get done.

Look at your work week as a FIVE-DAY WINDOW. Give yourself five days (Monday – Friday) to get all of that week's work done, and try not to move your work into next week where your time is already committed. The Command Central is made to be as flexible as our lives have to be. Give yourself some room to move something from Tuesday to Wednesday if need be. This takes the stress off having to stick to your original plan, but committing to Friday as your "drop dead date" for completing your work allows you to head into your weekend feeling like YOU EARNED IT!

WORK FROM HOME NOTES

WORK FROM HOME NOTES

WORK FROM HOME NOTES

WORK FROM HOME NOTES

Forget mistakes, forget failures,
forget everything,
except what you're going to do
now and do it.
Today is your lucky day.

— WILL DURANT

6

Declutter Your E-clutter!

Krista Parkinson is a pure champion at what she does. After graduating college, she began her Hollywood industry career as a "floater" at the William Morris Agency (now WME). There, she worked her way up to talent agent representing and finding jobs for creative people like hosts, actors, writers, producers, etc. She then went on to be vice president of Development for Tony Hawks' Production Company, 900 Films, and later as senior vice president of Business Development and Marketing for entertainment finance company Content Partners. She worked in the business, knows the business, and now has her own business, MyGrads-GetJobs—a personalized career-coaching company that empowers college students and recent graduates to target and land their first internships and jobs in the entertainment industry.

She's a star in my eyes. She's smart, sassy, direct, and really cares deeply about helping her clients (her kids, as she calls them) land in the job that they want, in an industry they hope to love.

And with all that she's got going, she's just exhausted. Depleted is the word she uses. At the end of each day, there's nothing left for herself. And during this COVID-19 lockdown, there's no delineation between work and play. (Sound familiar?) And what's play, other than walking the dog, or maybe a not-so-quick, physical-distancing obstacle-course-of-a-walk to the grocery store, right? She is super focused on her work, yet she spends way more time looking for things either in her inbox or on her desktop than she likes to admit. Until she did admit it, and decided it was time to course correct, get some systems set up, and indirectly prove that this COVID-19 thing could actually uncover some silver linings. Getting organized was #1 on her list.

Krista is certainly not alone in this challenge. And it doesn't matter whether you're a powerhouse like Krista, or maybe just a power condo— everyone can fall short in areas they're no expert in. Even with the killer assistant she has, the stuff that falls on her plate sometimes falls too deep for her liking. Like many of you, she feels overwhelmed by her inbox and declutter. While 500 or more emails in an inbox might stress one person out, 50 can do just the same for others. (Me, for instance, and Krista!)

This topic is critical no matter where you are working, but it is imperative now that you work at home since it's our number one vehicle for regular communication. And maybe it's the only communication you use, other than phones, of course. But even when/if you return to your office full or part-time, being able to easily navigate this technology world will do you a world of good. It will make you a more confident professional, a more self-reliant person. And who knows, being more comfortable with technology might allow you to connect better with your children. There's absolutely no downside, and only good can come of it.

Here's the deal about email. It's commonly the #1 stressor among people I work with when it comes to lost productivity. Like everything else that has real benefit, it can also be a real problem; whether it is an advantage or a stumbling block is in the way that you use it!

Here's the one really important thing that, if we'd all learned back in the 90s when email became a regular part of everyone's life, we wouldn't have nearly as many challenges with it as we do. Get ready—it's two words that can really change your life in relation to email if you get it and you let it. Your email inbox was/is only meant to be a **LOADING DOCK.** That's right...a LOADING DOCK! Nothing lives on a loading dock. A loading dock is a place for trains and trucks to temporarily drop off stuff that was in their compartments. But once they are unloaded there, they get moved to another place of residence. The dock is a space for loading and unloading, not a space for living or even hanging out for very long.

What do you do when your mail gets delivered to your house each day? I presume you go to the mailbox, take all the mail out, come into your house, and if you are like me, you head straight to the kitchen trash can or recycle bin to sort through the junk. After tossing what I don't need (which is most of it), I put Marty's mail in his mail slot and take mine to my office.

But picture this...you go down to your mailbox at the end of your driveway every afternoon and pull out just the mail you want and leave the rest in the mailbox. Then tomorrow, you do the exact same thing—only take out what you need or want. Keep doing this for a few weeks and not only will you have a mailbox filled with junk (or clutter), but you will also frustrate your mailman who might eventually stop delivering to you, especially if he has nowhere to put it! Funny how when it comes to our physical mail that's delivered, most of us clean out the box every day. But when it comes to our email inbox, we let mail live in there until either our company warns us we are headed toward maximum capacity so that purging is your only option, or the amount of emails is haunting you because of the strong probability that something is about to fall through the cracks, if it hasn't already.

Now you officially have what is referred to as **E-CLUTTER!**

How do we tackle our electronic clutter to ensure it never gets to the point at which it is a problem? How do we avoid having un-attended emails that lodge in your inbox, making you stressed out, defeated, overwhelmed, and headed to the refrigerator for ice cream? Well, we start with the same process we did for physical clutter and face every email in your inbox directly and promptly. Process, people, **PROCESS!**

Starting now, we are going to take the same processing steps with everything that comes into our inbox. Yes, the same steps we take for paper, we also take for email.

1. Let It Go

2. Let It Go to Someone Else

3. Do It Now

4. TO DO (Command Central)

5. TO SAVE (Folders)

But first, you need to set up places in your inbox for TO DO'S and TO SAVE'S.

Setting Up TO DO Folders:

COMMAND CENTRAL: (Sound familiar?)

Create a folder called **_COMMAND CENTRAL** under the word Inbox. If you type an underscore before the folder title, the computer automatically puts this folder first. Otherwise, it will appear alphabetically, and personally, I like these important folders that I use most frequently to be first. Under COMMAND CENTRAL, create a folder called **_ACTION THIS WEEK**. Next, one called **_NO DEADLINE**. Next, one titled **_AWAITING RESPONSE,** and the last one named **_WAITING TO READ** . These five folders that live under the heading COMMAND CENTRAL are where your TO DO'S live. Let's review each folder:

_COMMAND CENTRAL is just the heading; nothing lives in that folder.

_ACTION THIS WEEK: This is where you will drag all the emails that need to be followed up on now or in the very near future. It's where you are lining up your "to do's" to actually do them. These are the things that you have to do that take longer than 2 minutes and that need your further attention when you get to them.

_NO DEADLINE: These are the emails that relate to something that you may want to get to in the future, but there is no deadline. But you don't want to forget them, so they have a place to live. I go through this file once a week and remind myself what's in there. And often, I just decide then that I'm no longer interested in doing that, and I delete it.

_AWAITING RESPONSE: This is one of my very favorite files. When I reach out to someone to ask them to do something for me, and I want to be reminded that it's in their court, I blind copy myself on the email and then when it pops into my inbox, I drag it into this file. All the things I'm waiting for someone else to get back to me live in this file. I check it every day to remind me that I'm waiting for it. It's a brilliant file, if I do say so myself!

_WAITING TO READ: This is that file that I put all those articles, e-zines, and updates that I want to read, just not this very minute. I look at that file when I have some time to kill, and then I either toss the email when I'm finished reading it, or file it somewhere to save.

COMMAND CENTRAL IN EMAIL

Setting up TO SAVE folders:

You know that left side of your email inbox? Yup, that one. Well it's meant for folders to be set up, so you can easily and efficiently keep emails you want to refer to. So for instance, if you wanted to keep all the emails you get from me, you could either create a folder that says Wendy Ellin, or it could be called Professional Development, or it could be called Productivity. You have choices. Call it what you will most remember it by. But leaving it in your email inbox is just asking for trouble.

Here is what COMMAND CENTRAL looks like, as well as some basic ideas for email TO SAVE folders:

_COMMAND CENTRAL

_Action This Week

    _No Deadline

_Awaiting Response

_Waiting to Read

1. CLIENTS

    a. Existing Clients

    b. Past Clients

2. MARKETING

    a. Social Media

    b. Website

    c. Blogs

    d. Testimonials

    e. Creative

3. SPEAKING

    a. Speaking Materials

    b. Speaking Marketing

    c. Speaking Prospects

4. ADMIN

    a. VA

5. PROFESSIONAL DEVELOPMENT

    a. Coaches

6. MONEY

    a. Taxes

    b. Accounting

7. PERSONAL

    a. Ruby

    b. Travel

    c. Technology

    d. Health & Fitness

Everyone's job and life are different and unique to them and their distinct circumstances. Set your email inbox up to reflect your life and your job. Once you create these permanent electronic homes for emails, it's so easy to process. What's most important is that whatever you do, make sure it's easy enough for you to stay with it long enough to reap the benefits, or it will be a huge waste of time learning it and then ditching it shortly after.

Now with your TO DO folders and TO SAVE folders in place, you are ready to sort through your inbox and make one of five choices with every single email in there.

A quick note on sorting emails.

The easiest way to sort through your inbox is to **SORT BY SENDER.** I have found, as most of my clients have, that sorting by sender is the quickest way to get through all these emails you have built up in your inbox. Which, by the way, if I haven't said it loud enough...is just a **LOADING DOCK!** (Sorry, I just couldn't resist!) When sorting by sender, the computer automatically alphabetizes your emails based on who they are from. Then you scroll down, one person/name at a time (and there could be 130 emails from a person/name) and if you know you don't need any of the emails from Sue Avery, delete them all at once. If you need some of them, make one of five choices and keep going. You keep deleting from the senders you no longer need to keep until you come to a bunch of emails from Harry Mood that you want to keep. You have forty-six of them, but since he's head of HR, you may want to refer to them at some point in the future. So do one of two things here: either create a reference folder to the left of your inbox that says "Harry Mood" or one that says "HR." Your call. If you think you'll want to put other HR-related emails in there, then give Harry Mood his own folder. **YOU CAN'T HAVE TOO MANY FOLDERS.**

Quick review of five steps to take:

1. **Let It Go.** How do you let go of an email? Delete it.

2. **Let It Go To Someone Else**. How do you Delegate an email? Forward it.

3. **Do It Now**. Remember, that's the "two minutes or less" rule, so as emails come into your inbox, if you can pop them out into someone else's "court" in two minutes or less, just do it. During this de-clutter process, you can choose to either do all these now or drag them to your AWAITING MY RESPONSE folder to do when you have the time. It's all those quick emails that build up in your inbox that

you don't process and then at the end of the day, you have thirty emails that could have taken two minutes or less to respond to and now it's an hour of your time. *(I check my email at different times during my day for processing these exact ones—the ones I can get out of my inbox quickly. If you process even just a few "two minutes or less" emails throughout your day, you will have fewer emails in your inbox to deal with at the end of your day.)*

4. **TO DO Folder.** Your new COMMAND CENTRAL is your new best friend.

5. **TO SAVE Folder.** Simply click on an email or group of emails and drag them to the appropriate folder in your inbox.

WENDY'S WISDOM: Look at your life like a volleyball game. Your goal is to get as many balls (in this case emails) out of your court (inbox) as possible and into someone else's. I'm a big subscriber to this for three reasons:

1. I like processing and getting things out of my court to be productive.

2. I like responding to people who may be waiting for something from me, and if I can give it right back to them, I will.

3. People generally treat me the same way I treat them, so if I ask them for something they can get right back to me, they do.

Basic email tips for going forward with your new electronic COMMAND CENTRAL:

1. Remember that we are all in this together when it comes to the frustrating aspects of email.

2. Read your emails over before sending them—without the personal face-to-face communication, too many assumptions are derived from emails. Say what you want to say exactly like you would say it to them in person.

3. Get in and get out. Say what you need to and not another word more. Your "wall of words" is a promise the reader will not read all the way to the end and a guarantee he/she will miss the most important point you are trying to get through.

4. Only reply to the people who need to receive it.

5. Unsubscribe to at least five email lists per day. Deleting them will just make them go away for the day, but they'll be back in the morning! *(I unsubscribed to five lists every day this week and am amazed at how few emails I am now receiving.)*

6. Schedule times during your day for processing. We all agree that if all we did was sit in front of our computers all day and process email, we'd be plenty busy. But then when would our actual work get done? Focus on a project to completion, then check your email and do some processing for thirty minutes, then get back to work.

7. **REMEMBER THAT WE NEVER GET IT ALL DONE!** The minute we process all our email and leave our desk to go to the bathroom, there are seventeen more emails in our inbox when we return. That's life—for all of us. Don't sweat it. Do as much as you can, put the rest in a place when you need to see it next, and go enjoy your life.

ORGANIZING YOUR DESKTOP

What's your desktop look like? For most, that's another technology nightmare. Tons of icons that all look the same floating on your screen. No wonder it takes you so long to find things. Here it comes again...how's that working for you? If it's all good, keep them there. If not, let's organize them as well.

Create one folder on your desktop that says WLE. Those are my initials; you use yours. Then in that folder lives everything else. So when I open that, here are the categories:

- ► CLIENTS
- ► ADMIN
- ► MARKETING
- ► SPEAKING
- ► PHOTOS
- ► ARTWORK
- ► PROF DEVELOPMENT
- ► WENDY/PERSONAL

And from there, I create subfolders to put documents in. So these folder names mirror those in my inbox. It takes way less time to click open the PHOTOS file and find a headshot I'm looking for than scouring the desktop of multiple duplicate icons to find what I'm looking for. And to me, it doesn't make sense. So take the time to save time later. That's my JAM.

DESKTOP FOLDERS

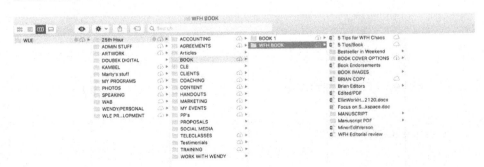

ORGANIZE YOUR PHONE

Want to organize your iPhone? Most people organize their apps by subject, which I totally get. But I still don't want 6 pages of apps in folders. So I have all my apps on page one. How? By creating folders according to their color, not their subject. Because truthfully, that's how I remember them. I know Uber is black, What's App is green, my bank is red, Delta is blue, etc. If what you have isn't working, try the color method. It's been a game changer for me (and for Krista too!).

ORGANIZED IPHONE APPS

So there you have it. Your life is waiting for you, and with having easy systems for processing emails and navigating your desktop and iPhone, you should be well on your way to getting work done with less stress and more joy.

When Krista and I are on our weekly Zoom calls (yes, I taught her my systems, but she insists on weekly accountability, and as she likes to say, "weekly handholding"), she's setting up her email inbox and I'm just on the other end keeping her accountable. Turns out she's not doing it unless I'm "there" with her, and for now, Zoom is as good as it gets. As she's going through her emails while sharing her screen, I happen to glance at an email from Mark Cuban that says, "Sure, I'll be a guest at Coffee with KP. When?"

"WHHHAAATTT? You know Mark Cuban well enough to get an email from him? Okay, do tell me more," I say.

She has a podcast called Coffee with KP where she invites industry professionals as guests for a virtual coffee chat to find out what they do, how they do it, and any advice they would give those just starting out. As it happens, she used to work for Mark, and I just so happened to see the email as it came in. This is where I confess to Krista that I'm really not a stalker of all things Hollywood. It's just that my dad was a writer for TV back in the 70s and 80s, for shows like *Hart to Hart*, *The Jeffersons*, *The Good Times*, *The Love Boat*, *Trapper John MD*, *Alice*, and his claim to fame was *Dukes of Hazzard*. So I love hearing her stories from her past foray in that lane. It was one of those "Get outta here, no you get outta here" moments that still crack me up when I think about it.

Needless to say, Krista is cranking. She's not only working the systems, but she actually invited me, yes, little old me, to be a guest speaker on one of her Coffee with KP podcasts. Go figure...Mark Cuban and Wendy Ellin getting invited to the same classroom...there is a God!

WRITE THIS DOWN:

1. Set up your electronic COMMAND CENTRAL NOW!

2. Set up, or re-organize, your TO SAVE folders so they make sense to you, with zero duplication.

3. Sort by sender and process everything in your inbox, using the newly set up folder system.

4. Do two processing sessions each day by moving things where you need them next, not by stopping your work to answer an email.

5. Clean up your desktop by mirroring the same folders in your email.

6. Set up your iPhone apps according to color so they all remain on the front screen.

WORK FROM HOME NOTES

WORK FROM HOME NOTES

WORK FROM HOME NOTES

WORK FROM HOME NOTES

*Human beings are not born
once and for all on the day
their mothers give birth to
them, but...life obliges them
over and over again to give
birth to themselves.*

— GABRIEL GARCIA MARQUEZ

7

Kids, Partners, and Pets, Oh My!

There are a ton of books out there solely dedicated to the subject of multitasking. I've read quite a few of them, and I am not convinced by any argument that suggests multitasking is productive, pleasurable, or even possible! And due to this work-from-home reality, we all must deal with the issue of multiple, simultaneous demands on an entirely new level. No matter whether you have dogs, partners, kids, adult kids, parents, neighbors—you name it, the level of distractions bombarding us on a daily basis is real. And the constant interruptions are a huge deterrent to staying focused on our work, which is, after all, how we earn the income that allows us to support the critical needs of our lives. Trying to accomplish any one thing is a challenge: trying to achieve everything thrown at us at the same time would demand superhuman skills.

Most people think they can earn a badge of honor for multitasking. And here it comes again... "How's that working for you?" **Trying to accomplish multiple tasks simultaneously doesn't increase your efficiency or productivity, and it clearly doesn't make you feel good about yourself or your work product.**

And these days, nowhere is there a more heightened awareness of this struggle than from those now working from home. Meet my client Monica. She's now totally moved her work into her home (challenge #1)—a home where not only her husband is present during the day (challenge #2), because he works a night shift, but her three kids are also now there doing the home school thing (challenge #3, #4 and #5). Just like the rest of the world, right? Let the games begin!

Her 13- and 12-year-old are pretty self-sufficient. They get to their school work, and have no trouble finding things to keep them out of trouble. However, her 4-year-old, Christian, is autistic and has special needs (challenge #6). These challenges are easy to identify on paper, yet hard to address, much less overcome. And when you live them, they are very, very real. And not just for Monica. I know that more readers than not share some peculiar-to-you challenge every day, something that is either more obvious or more problematic now that everyone vies for time, space and attention under the same roof all day, every day.

So Monica is in a client Zoom meeting, about to present her part, when Christian goes into a full-blown meltdown. Screaming at the top of his well-tuned-up lungs, not willing or able to move, to stop, to do anything. Monica panics. It's about to be her turn to present. But that's just not possible with what's going on in her background. So she says to her Zoom attendees, "Listen, I'm so sorry, but my son is autistic, and he's having a meltdown that I really need to give my attention to right now." At which point, her client responds, "I totally get it, as I also have a son with autism. Let's just all take a minute and see if Monica can get him to calm down." *Thank God,* she thinks to herself and she walks away from the computer, grabs her son, puts him on her lap and all remains quiet on the Monica front.

And that's just the morning's event. That afternoon, Monica gets a call from her brother who runs a dog boarding business. He has 12 dogs in his house that he's looking after for the week. But her brother's wife goes into labor, and he needs to do something with all these dogs. So he asks Monica and their other siblings to each take 3 dogs for the next few days while he leaves to welcome his child into the world. Although some of us might find a way to say no, she says yes. Now she has three strange dogs in her house, and one of them is an exotic Israeli dog who only responds to commands in Arabic. So she not only gets the dog, but it comes with a list of Arabic commands she needs to use with him. Honestly, I couldn't make this s*#t up if I wanted to!

Needless to say, everyone has their own level of cray-cray in their home. It's new, it's challenging, it changes by the minute, and you just have to go with it.

Let me say that again...YOU JUST HAVE TO GO WITH IT. How do you do that—how do you do everything that needs to be done and still breathe, still honor your commitment to your work and your marriage, your kids, and oh, there's you? Is it by multitasking? I'm thinking not.

Actually, "switch-tasking," as Dave Crenshaw refers to in his book *The Myths of Multitasking,* is what we are actually talking about here. And switch-tasking is exactly how to describe what we all do all day long.

You're on your computer cranking out a project that is due this afternoon by close of business. The doorbell rings; it's the delivery guy needing your signature for a package you ordered on Amazon 3 months ago (because it's coming from China, and the one thing that's slowed down since COVID-19 is package delivery times). On your way back to your computer, which for now is set up at your kitchen island counter, you see your 9-year-old watching a video on his iPad instead of doing his school assignment. So you spend 7 minutes getting him back to his work (4 of those minutes for negotiating). Now you're back at your computer when an email comes in from American Express' Fraud Department suggesting there may be a problem with your card. Call at once, before someone goes haywire on Amazon!

While you're on hold with Amex, you get a text asking if you can move the 1 pm Zoom call up to noon. REALLY? Yup, really. Oh, and BTW, what was I doing when the doorbell rang? HELP!

In an instant, all these interruptions are fighting for your attention that a mere twenty-five minutes ago did not even exist. And now you are trying to juggle all of them at the same time, while making sure you give everything and everyone the ATTENTION THEY NEED AND DESERVE.

In the age of working from home, here are some suggestions for how to create some systems for success around this challenge:

1. Huddle with your "home team" every morning to talk about what the day looks like for everyone living under your roof. If you and your partner are in charge of the kids, then determine who's doing what relative to their care/supervision. Just for today. And if necessary, break it down into the morning hours (8a-12noon) and then afternoon (12-6pm), whatever works for you, but don't start the day without this meeting. It will be more important than any Zoom meeting you attend. This is your "home team." Talk to them, make a plan, take it by the hour, and readjust as necessary. Your goal is to get as many work sessions in as possible, while making sure everyone else gets what they need.

2. Ground rules are the JAM! Set them up, put them on the refrigerator, hang a white board on the pantry door—do whatever it takes to make sure everyone sees them. Then get everyone's input. Your "home team" will be much more inclined to give you what you need if you give them what they need. They could look this:

   ▶ No interrupting while on the phone/Zoom call unless you're bleeding or can't breathe.

- ▶ Ask for what you want long before you want it, not the minute before if at all possible.
- ▶ Take your dirty dishes to the sink No exceptions.
- ▶ If you want a snack, take one. You don't need permission.
- ▶ Walk the dog when it's your time to. Or switch with someone else, but the dog needs to go and doesn't care who takes her.
- ▶ Schoolwork comes before video games. So make sure you are prepared to show me your work, before you hop on that iPad.

3. Strengthen your parenting muscles. I know, sounds nuts, right? But being a mom and being a parent are two different things. Mom drops the kids off at school with a kiss, and heads to work knowing their kid is taken care of for the day. But the parent is the one who says, "I have a meeting and cannot be disturbed for the next hour. When I'm done, you get my attention for the next 15 minutes, so be thinking about how you want to use them!" If you need to hear this again, please know that setting limits and honoring them are excellent parenting skills, good for both you and your children.

4. Ask the adults in the house for the same considerations as the kids. Look, distractions are distractions, no matter the age. If your husband wants to watch his crime show while eating lunch, ask him to go upstairs and do it so you don't have to hear it in the background.

5. Use the commute time you no longer have to accommodate your "home team." This will ensure that work hours can be reserved for work sessions. Give them what they want early or late in the day, and they will give you what you need during peak work hours.

6. Take breaks to check in with your "home team." Is everyone good? Does everyone have what they need for the next hour or two? Check-ins will help you stay focused without wondering when the next interruption will occur. And it will occur, so just expect it to.

7. I suggest starting work-related zoom meetings with 5-minute check-ins to share anything that might come up while on the call. If I know that my kid is going to wake up from a nap, and there's a chance I might need to attend to that, I think sharing that is key to setting expectations up front. Look, we are all experiencing the same sense of dislocation, maybe in different degrees, but most work colleagues will offer a level of latitude or forgiveness that might not have been even considered before. So being transparent about what's going on in your house during this hour isn't unlike what's going on in the rest of the meeting attendees' lives. As I said, we all have our own level of cray-cray. Share yours with me, and I might just feel a whole lot better about my own!

Now that you've lined up your "home team" schedule, let's talk about focusing when you're actually in your work sessions. Dr. T. Jackson from Loughborough University, in his article entitled *Breaking Bad Habits: The Negative Effect of Email and Instant Messaging on the Workplace*, found that it takes 64 seconds to retrieve your train of thought after an interruption by email. That means if you check your inbox every five minutes, you waste 8.5 hours a week. My guess is that it takes just as long to retrieve your train of thought after an interruption by ANYTHING! So if possible, stop letting it—whatever "it" is—interrupt you!

How? I so often hear the expression, "The only things we can be certain of are death and taxes." But in reality, we don't have to pay our taxes, right? That's a choice we get to make. The more realistic version of that would be..."The only thing that we can be certain of is death...and making choices." So in light of that, let's start getting better at the choices we make. Begin with the ones that seem small, like whether to answer that phone or to start that conversation that you think may only take fifty seconds, but in actuality, it takes fifty minutes.

The dictionary's definition of FOCUS is *"a point upon which attention, activity, etc., is directed or concentrated.*" Really? Can you imagine in our current work-from-home reality—with all our never-ending distractions—doing something like having a conversation with your teenager and not also paying attention to the coronavirus update on the TV in the background? Or how about gazing at the microwave to see how many seconds it has left until done and trying to acknowledge your youngest child as he shares his art project with you ALL AT THE SAME TIME? Research shows that the average person loses focus six to ten times per minute! In fact, I'd venture a guess that six to ten times is somewhat of a low number. We exist in the bottomless pit of attention-grabbing opportunities 24/7/365. The only way to avoid it is to go to sleep...or to set up your life so that it is possible not to have so many options in front of you at once. Turn multitasking, or switch-tasking, into UNI-TASKING for the sake of sanity, productivity, and a little self-control!

So here's what I propose for every work session:

1. Commit to the process of completion. That's right, your goal is to set a short- or long-term goal for completing a project. If you get to your laptop in the morning and you know that you have a deadline of COB (close of business) that day, how many hours can you plan on devoting to that project today? Break it down into a morning session and an afternoon session if your day requires you to tackle other things. You get to make the choice as to how you spend your time every day. Choose it wisely and set yourself up for satisfaction and accomplishment, not frustration and failure.

2. Start communicating to your team/boss at work that you are trying to increase your daily efficiency and productivity in this new work-from-home reality, and in doing so, you are asking for their support in seeing your work to completion before focusing on the next matter that needs your attention.

3. Make some (at least one) of your work sessions "uninterruptible" every day. Let your home team know when that is. Put a red light bulb in a lamp near you. When the red light is on, that's when you cannot be interrupted. When it's off, you can be. That means make yourself available for your home team at the end of your red light work session. And with work peeps, letting them know that you are in a red light work session might just get them to do the same. If everyone has uninterruptible time to do their work, then no one is being interrupted.

4. Or if you have a door to your home office, put a *PLEASE DO NOT DISTURB* sign on your door asking that you not be disturbed. Better yet, put a PLEASE DO NOT DISTURB UNTIL _____, including a time at which you will be available to them. Then honor that time.

5. Remember that UNITASKING (working on one thing at a time) directly improves the quality of your work. Multitasking not only slows you down when it comes to productivity, but it increases the chances of error, which ultimately increases the time it takes for completion when you find yourself having to re-do your work.

6. Schedule appointments with yourself (see block times below). Crazy as it sounds, if you block time out on your calendar every week to focus on your work, not only will you be more inclined to stay focused, but you will start to look forward to that time block where you can get substantial amounts of work completed. It's your time for whatever you want—even if it's for email processing, returning phone calls, or tying up loose ends.

BLOCK TIMES:

I commit to having 3 block times on my calendar per week. That means I have certain times blocked on my calendar to actually get my work done. Here's what they are:

1. **Maximize Monday:** This first block time is for assessing my upcoming week. It's for making sure that if something is due that I need to work on, it takes priority. It's for making sure that if I have a Zoom lunch planned for Thursday, I connect with the person I'm "dining" with to make sure it's still good for them. I look at my week and adjust it as necessary so I have a more realistic picture of the week ahead. That's every Monday morning.

2. **CRAP DAY**: Friday afternoon is reserved for all the crap I put off all week until Friday. Some things just land in this block time that I always do on Friday afternoon, like correspondence, entering contacts into my database, creating invoices, etc. Other projects that I need to wrap up that don't take mega brain power get tossed in that time as well. It's just my time to close out my week with as much productivity as possible. For me, there's nothing like going into my weekend feeling like I earned it!

3. **"Floater" Block Time:** This block time changes every week depending on what I have going on. If I'm on back-to-back Zoom calls on Wednesday, then my "floater" block time has to be either Tuesday or Thursday. Regardless of when it happens, my rule of thumb is that I can reschedule a weekly block time, but I'm not allowed to cancel it altogether. This ensures that I have designated times every week to get my work done.

Look, this is all new for so many of us. Where before our time was being used up with round-trip commutes, travel to client meetings, out-of-town travel, client entertainment, and a host of other time suckers that went out when COVID-19 entered our lives, we may actually have more say in our God-given 24 hours a day than ever before. So before we wrap this chapter, let's outline how those hours might be used so we can get the most out of this lemon-of-a-year we're living in:

1. Try like crazy to set a realistic schedule for the day, and then honor it. Maybe you break your 8 hours up into 3, 3, and 2. Maybe you start at 10 and finish at 9 pm. But in between, you take a hike with your dog, or kid, or both. Maybe you start each day with 30 minutes of a social Zoom over coffee. Ask your work team how they are working in their home to see if you can create a schedule that's in sync. The key is to do what works for you, as long as you get your work done. Or perhaps go balls-to-the-wall from 8am to 6 pm, and then shut it down. One of the biggest challenges I've heard from those I've interviewed is the lack of delineation between work and play. But that's because you're not creating it. Stop trying to find it, and instead create it. If you're missing the feeling of accomplishment when leaving your old office after a killer productive day, then do the disconnecting right there in your work-from-home space. You'll feel just as accomplished, if not more.

2. Speaking of working out...get your body moving! Even if you convert your commute time to exercise, 30 minutes is all you need. Get outside, hop on a bike, do a 30-minute taped routine, whatever works for you. But this sitting all day at the computer is just not anyone's idea of fun, healthy, or productive. Maybe you're longing for that commute home where you get to decompress after the day. Make your exercise/walk time right after disconnecting your decompression time.

3. Make sure to schedule time in between Zoom calls to avoid Zoom-itis. We're all dealing with this, so speaking to it will be no surprise to anyone. Someone is waiting for you to say this because they're thinking it as well. Be the one.

4. If walking to the local coffee shop around the corner will change

things up for you, and it's safe to do so, go for it. Just having something as simple as that to look forward every day is necessary for your energy, your sanity, and the mere pleasure of someone else making coffee for you!

Your days will start to look the same, unless you make sure they don't. So take it one day at a time. Get your home team on board. Share your home-team plan with your work team. Keep an open mind and your sense of humor intact. Because if nothing else, we've sure learned how handy that comes in.

Now, back to Monica. She's doing exactly that—taking each day as it comes. She's meeting with her home team every morning, using her red lamp, practicing transparency wherever and whenever necessary, and finding a way to get her work done while zooming, texting, mommying, parenting, and training an exotic Arabic dog to *arqad* (lay down in Arabic).

WRITE THIS DOWN!

1. Have a home team meeting every day.

2. Set ground rules and display them for everyone to see.

3. Be a parent, not just a mom/dad.

4. Take breaks/move your body/get outside.

5. Be transparent.

6. Uninterrupted work sessions are your friend.

7. Plan 3 block times on your calendar each week for getting work done.

8. Disconnect!

9. Say, "NO, thank you," when asked if you can keep 3 strange dogs, even if for 1 day, much less many.

WORK FROM HOME NOTES

WORK FROM HOME NOTES

WORK FROM HOME NOTES

WORK FROM HOME NOTES

Find the perfection in every moment instead of trying to make every moment perfect.

— DONNALYNN CIVELLO

8

Just Get Out of Your Own Flippin' Way

There are a few self-defeating behaviors that, despite any attempts we make to rid ourselves of, somehow seem to creep back into our being. I won't spend too much time on any of these for two reasons. One is that there is so much research devoted to these subjects that reading a book solely dedicated to each would offer you far greater insight than I offer here. And second, I'm sticking with my theory that what we focus on expands. And since none of these issues are ones I'm interested in you keeping around, I'll touch lightly for the sake of reminding you to address them directly and to get them promptly behind you. Give their history of keeping you ineffective/unproductive as little attention as you can. Be in charge of your behaviors: when you stop allowing them to dictate your responses to possible roadblocks, you will no longer need to give them attention.

PROCRASTINATING:. Working from home is "working" Alan a bit differently than those who are made anxious by the environmental changes. Alan is a lawyer, has projects that have not quite been completed, and he knows that finishing them and clearing space (emotionally, and especially in his tightly packed house, physically) for the new ones coming in would be smart, on many levels. The reason, he says, that he can't seem to get closure on the existing projects is consistent with what I hear from some people who now work from home every day, who no longer travel for business or pleasure, who in large part only communicate on a screen: every day sort of seems like the one before. There is no week, there is no weekend, there is no sense of distinction and there is no sense of urgency. Alan does not especially like the lagging projects, and figures if he doesn't get it done today, well, there is tomorrow, or a week from tomorrow—who can tell the difference anymore?

Procrastination has many reasons, and many excuses. It's common to all, a universal behavior, but ultimately it does not serve you well. There are at least a handful of reasons why we procrastinate even knowing and admitting we shouldn't, all of them easy to use as an excuse, yet none of them valid. And the interesting thing about procrastinating is that most of the time, the task we are putting off is not nearly as bad as we think. Here's the key...it's the STARTING of the task that we can't seem to get to, not the completion of the task. And you must *begin* to be able to *conclude*, hence the trouble.

The easiest solution for no longer putting things off is to commit to the starting of a project first. Put a date/time on your calendar when nothing else can get in the way of your starting, and if necessary, only bite off the project bits at a time. Remember, you just need to start it, or start the next piece, not necessarily finish it then.

I recall when working in radio sales that each fall I had to come up with a sales budget for the upcoming year—it was clearly the singular thing I disliked most in that job. So after many years of putting it off until the day before it was due and staying up nearly all night to complete it, I decided to split my client list into quarters and only tackle one quarter per night until, after four nights, the budget was complete. Or at least it was a good starting point. I tackled the first piece to the best of my ability, then the next piece the next night and so on, and after parceling it out like I finally did, the project wasn't anywhere near the obstacle it initially appeared to be. Now don't get me wrong, I didn't all of a sudden love this project, but it no longer had a hold on me like it had in the past. It was an inevitable part of my job that, once I had a plan, worked well enough to repeat over the years.

I am also big on rewards. That's right, arrange a reward for yourself, any kind of reward, for getting to something that appeared painful at the onset but that you started anyway. If a gold star on the wall at work or a late night out with the girls used to be your rewards, create a new system, closer to home. Give yourself a pat on the back and an hour to take your puppy to the park if that is what you enjoy. Head to Starbucks for that afternoon Frappuccino. Whatever it is, make it worth the effort to get into that project you keep putting off—MAKE A DENT and it will make a difference.

PERFECTIONISM: When I told client Allyson about the do-it-in-pieces-when-necessary approach, she reacted strongly. "I could never do that. I need to have the whole of my work in front of me so that I can edit, re-shape, manage and control it until it is perfect." Perhaps you can guess that the work I did with Allyson—-who crafted her work project to perfection but was terribly unhappy at her work—was to understand what the insistence on perfection—and the resulting depression when she did not achieve it—was doing to her life.

Perfection. What a difficult concept to try to live up to. What an unreasonable goal for most projects. What an impossible standard to be demanded to honor. And yet...what a worthy goal to strive for! NOT!

The trick here is to strive for excellence, but after you have done your very best, to accept your humanity. By that I mean appreciate and accept the strongest result you can produce, even if it is not perfect.

I'm a huge subscriber to this quote I frequently use when coaching my clients and when raising my girls...

"Don't let the PERFECT get in the way of the GOOD."

For me, if it represents the most that I can produce after setting myself up for success and fully focusing on the project (as we learned strategies for in previous chapters), my best is good enough. Or better yet, let's make GREAT the new PERFECT! This way, GREAT will not only be attainable (unlike PERFECT), but it's a much better use of my time and energy than fretting about not being PERFECT. Most of my days are filled with positive, engaging, productive experiences that I conclude are great. And that's just good enough for me!

As I spend more time in a business turned on its side by the recent events, I see an increasing number of people who, quite honestly, just don't have time for perfection. They have been asked to do more with less, and they are just trying to keep afloat and get control of their lives the best they know how. They fret that their work product will diminish because the volume of requests for their time and talent is increasing, and their resources are diminishing. What a *perfect* time to remember two things:

1.   Organize the many tasks coming at you the best you can. Take to heart the advice of the previous chapters about how to prioritize, how to delegate, how to respond to interruptions, etc., and prepare yourself as well as possible to do great work.

2.   Great work is to be celebrated. This is NOT to say you or those you work with should lower your sights or accept a work product that is beneath you or that is not all that you can achieve. But it is a strong message that sometimes you must take pride and pleasure in a product that is less than the perfect you tried to reach. One more thought: people who strive only for perfection can never be totally satisfied with anything less, and the ongoing battle that reality creates only sets them up for failure on some level.

WORKAHOLISM: Edward had been raised to see himself as a reflection of his work. As a result, he did very little of anything else. He could not understand why he had trouble in relationships, and he came to me to make sure those wouldn't suffer anymore due to transitioning to a home-based work space. In my work with him, he made it clear that he also wanted help in being even more successful at work, thinking it would make him successful everywhere else. The message here is an obvious one but one that seems hard to embrace: if you give everything to any one facet of your life, the rest of your life will wither from inattention.

The siren song of "stay longer and do more" at the job is impossible for most of us to ignore. But if you are worn down, if you have tried to accomplish too many things and never take a break or have the chance to do discrete pieces of your work as well as possible—if you are just *tapped out*—you risk having nothing to give to your job, your family, yourself. (And by the way, if you don't start putting yourself first, everything else WILL SUFFER.) When your mental and physical health is at risk from not being able to control your drive to work, you are literally left with nothing to actually work with. And eventually, that is what most workaholics are faced with. They are worn out, energy-depleted, too depressed to be effective in their work, and much less productive. Suffice it to say that there is so much more to life than work, no matter what you do.

I feel incredibly blessed to do something in this world that I am completely 100% passionate about—to the point where it doesn't feel like work and I could do it all day long. But even having said that, we (including myself) all need a break in the action—any action. Change and some recharging time are essential to maintaining a clear, focused path from which to create whatever your passion is in this world.

As it happens, Alan, Allyson, and Edward are "getting with the program." This new work-from-home experience has them each reevaluating what's important. As we all should be. As of this writing, I just lost a cousin due to COVID-19. And while it didn't need to hit this close to home for me to understand the magnitude of why we are all working from home to begin with, it certainly puts it all in perspective. It's random, it's deadly, and it's real. So hug the family you're sheltering with, and let gratitude be what leads you going forward.

Start to look at where some of these self-defeating behaviors stick out in your life. Are you a major procrastinator? If so, make a list of the tasks you are procrastinating. Put each one on a 3x5 Action Card and then place that card in your Command Central on the day you plan to start that item. That's a great first step, and you have to start somewhere!

Is the desire for perfect getting in the way of your good or great? If so, spend some time visualizing what outcome you could be really satisfied with and make that your end goal. Don't call it anything, just see it in its final state. That might make the journey to get there more enjoyable and attainable.

For those of you who find yourselves leaning toward workaholic behavior, read Chapter 7 again! And make sure to use those break times I speak about to do something that requires a different part of your brain function. Take a walk, play with the dog, hang with your kid—anything to change things up for you to break the "work" cycle you're on and can't seem to get off. Daily breaks in work will avoid the burnout, energy depletion, and increased stress you may commonly experience.

In short...Get To It, Let Great Be Good Enough, and remember that Too Much of Any One Thing isn't always the answer!

WRITE THIS DOWN!

1. Stop procrastinating by getting started, one small step at a time.

2. Don't let the perfect get in the way of good/great.

3. Integrate play into work to avoid burnout.

4. Focus on gratitude every day.

WORK FROM HOME NOTES

WORK FROM HOME NOTES

WORK FROM HOME NOTES

WORK FROM HOME NOTES

*To be trusted is a greater
compliment than to be loved.*

— GEORGE MacDONALD

9

Because I Said I Would

Marty and I have this wonderful home in Atlanta. It's tucked back in the woods behind a house that sits on the street. So we feel like we live in the north Georgia mountains, when in reality, we are right on the edge of midtown Atlanta. It's completely the best of both worlds: total privacy, views of nature outside every window, and an interior space we created that's pure joy. It's a place that's welcomed so many visitors over the years. A few years ago, we had a good friend stay with us who was in the process of getting divorced. As it happens, our home has been a landing place for several people getting ready to launch their next chapter. And while we don't always encourage the split-ups, we are delighted to offer our place when needed.

Meg was staying with us for about 3-4 weeks. She would leave for work early in the am before I was even up, and sometimes she didn't come home until dark. She had one of those "your work runs your life" jobs; she was pretty burnt out but was sticking it out. Too many changes at once wasn't her idea of a good time.

Every evening I asked her if she'd be joining us for dinner the next day. Most days it was, "No, thank you. Too busy." One day, I happened to be going to the grocery store, and told her if she would be coming home by dinner time (which was flexible), we'd love her to join us. She said, "Yes, I'll be home no later than 7:30." Okay, cool. So dinner time rolled around, and I was cooking (not my jam at all, but willing and able, sort of). Marty got home around 7, and by 7:30, but there was no Meg. 8 pm, no Meg and no call from Meg. Hmmm…What's a starving host to do?

Well, this was the first time it happened during her stay, but certainly not the last.

All of the topics we discussed thus far are central to the way I live my life with purpose, balance, and peace of mind. They are almost as fundamental to my daily existence as breathing, sleeping and eating. But none of them resonates more with me on a personal or professional level than the subject of **BEING ON TIME**. And you'll notice that this is a subject rarely spoken about in daily conversation, unless you attend a specific session devoted to it.

It is rather amazing how many times in my life I have waited way past the scheduled appointment time for friends, clients, family members, and total strangers. I would venture to say that most of us spend an inordinate amount of time in our life just WAITING FOR SOMEONE. And honestly, it's not the waiting that stirs the emotional stuff up in me, but the fact that my time is not being respected from the one imposing the wait. I try to recognize that the people who are late are frequently kind and loving people who would never purposely disrespect me. However, their insensitivity when only considering their own agendas directly affects not only my time but my attitude and opinion about their ability to honor their word. And in my opinion, being credible and honoring your word are the silent, yet essential, core values needed to maintain a relationship where truth, respect and integrity are the foundation.

Now I have a role to play in this promptness dance, as we all do. This is when *making choices* comes back into play (as it does in virtually every interaction). We don't actually have to do nothing while we wait for those whose moral compass and time management skills don't match ours. And actually, we don't have to wait either! I use this time (when leaving isn't my choice) to delve into my **WAITING TO READ** file we spoke about in Chapter 5. Always presuming I will have a wait when going places, I just find a way to use that time to my advantage.

Working from home, I spend more than half my day on Zoom calls, either in group meetings, 1:1 coaching sessions, interviewing potential clients, or just connecting with friends. After all, how else can we connect with our loved ones if we cannot see them live? And I'm pretty astounded at the number of meetings in which I am waiting for the attendee/s to join me. And the driving time we once had to contend with (because let's face it, isn't traffic the culprit every time?) has been replaced with barking dogs, whining kids, run-on Zoom meetings, home-schooling and anything else keeping us from showing up. And that's just it. How you show up is how you show up. How you do anything is how you do everything.

I ask you right now to grab a pen and paper and write down all the people in your life who are chronically late. I have no doubt that you will easily come up with five people, either in your personal or professional life, who fit that bill. Yes? (What is most amazing is not how many names you can come up with, but how fast those names will pop into your head!) Maybe you are one of them? Think about that for a minute!

I have people I love in my life who are stubbornly resistant to growing a new understanding about the importance of this issue. Frequently, when Marty and I are dressing to entertain certain friends on a Saturday night (pre-COVID), I find myself in the closet thinking and sharing under my breath, but loud enough for him to hear me, "Don't hurry, they're never here on time." And here's the reality about this...no matter what else is true about these people, they are labeled as "late," and it impacts my relationship with them. ***WE EARN OUR REPUTATION EITHER WAY!*** You will ultimately have a reputation of being an on-time person or a late person—and the difference is this: having the reputation of being a late person doesn't require much effort on your part. But being an on-time person not only takes effort, it takes TIME. Your time. And it's worth that effort and the investment of your time!

My clients will often moan, "You mean I have to have more time just to be on time? I don't have enough time in my day as it is, and you want me to have more?" And the answer is YES. Because in order to be on time, you have to actually think about it. Winging it won't work. Sounds simple in theory, but it's somewhat more difficult in reality, especially if you are new to changing this habit. More on this in a minute.

Timeliness is an issue that always involves two parties: those who are late and those doing the waiting for those who are late. And for many, the question of respect never comes up. I think that this is the way they have always navigated through their days and are not even attuned to how it may affect others, because being timely is not a conversation we tend to have often, lightly or directly for the sake of courtesy or respect, much less reputation!

I remember when I was selling radio back in the early 90s. I had several clients who were in Buford, Georgia, which was at least forty-five minutes from either my home or the radio station. The common question for me was, "Do I call the client to confirm my appointment with them and take the chance that they will cancel it if I do, or just drive out there and hope that they remember the appointment and are actually present?" My dilemma was whether I honor my commitment to show up on time, even at the too-common risk of the client not honoring his word. Having my client fail to appear was not only frustrating, but it was a bad use of my time and energy, not to mention my car. But that frustration was no match for my word—I came when promised because I said I would!

So back to Meg. I decided to share my thoughts on this subject in a way she could hear me. This email below followed our open and honest discussion about not what *I* wanted out of her being on time, but what *she* could potentially experience. Here she shares her thoughts and experience since adapting a **BE ON TIME** attitude and a new way of living. I'm not sure I could put it in words better than she.

I juggle a lot of balls in my day, I over commit, and most of the time, I under perform in the context of being on time. Recently, Wendy pointed out to me that your reputation with respect to timeliness precedes you and often defines how others perceive you in far-reaching ways. Her comments resonated and made me realize that I did not want to be known as a person who is never on time, who consequently is seen as someone who doesn't respect other people's time, and who is frantically rushing from place to place. I did not want to continue to be someone who begins each encounter apologizing for being late.

I made a decision to change, and it has profoundly impacted how I move through my day and my relationships with others. It is an unexpected feeling of freedom and one that merits sharing. All it took was a few simple steps (with Wendy's guidance) and some self-awareness to do things differently.

First, I had a terrible habit of trying to tie up loose ends before leaving my home or office: I would make a few phone calls, shoot off a couple of emails, take out the trash, and tidy up. While those things may have been important to do, I always waited until the last minute to do them and they always took longer than I had planned.

Next, I realized that I had no concept of how long it took to get out of my house or office, then to my car, and then to the place I need to be. I never took into consideration things like traffic, events going on in the city which cause congestion on the road, or that I needed to build in time to familiarize myself with a place, route, or area I have never been to before. I have made the decision to think about these considerations and leave myself plenty of time to get where I am going.

Now, rather than aggressively driving to get to places on time or to fill my headspace with what I was going to tell the person to justify my tardiness, I now enjoy being in the car. I listen to my favorite tunes, and I have the appropriate headspace to prepare myself for my arrival at whatever meeting or appointment I am on my way to. Before, it would take me several minutes once I arrived to just decompress from the frantic and rushed experience of getting there. I couldn't really be fully present once I got to where I was going because I was still unraveling the unnecessary energy that was forced upon me because of my poor planning.

People have taken notice of the change, and while that feels good, it feels even better to know that it was possible to change and to take simple steps to being a more thoughtful and mindful person about how my time impacts me and others.

Wow! Not only did she get it, but it was no longer than a few days after our initial discussion when she shared this awareness with me, which means it didn't take long to acknowledge, accept, and consciously correct the problem. And as she shared above, the positive implications it immediately had on her life not only served as ongoing incentive, but also provided the good feeling she longed for that will ultimately change her reputation. I'd say that's a win/win...don't you think?

Nothing about the importance of being prompt, and being known for honoring your word, changes because the location of your office has changed. Even from home, there are some things you can do immediately that will not only enhance good feelings as you move through your day, but they will ensure that you are no longer identified in the "late" category again. Yes, there will always be circumstances you cannot avoid. But if you replace your reputation with "on time" instead of "late," not only will you not feel as bad when the unavoidable circumstance is upon you, but those waiting for you will look at it, and you, differently.

1. Decide that you are going to be "ON TIME." That means whatever it takes, you are in. NOT half in. FULLY 100% in. Start seeing yourself on time for every Zoom meeting, every in-person engagement, everywhere you go. Even see yourself early with time to process your email while waiting for others to arrive. Or better yet just enjoy the few extra minutes in your day to do nothing. What a concept!

2. If you find yourself the one on the waiting side, consider having a conversation with those in your life whose tardiness impedes your relationship by disallowing the authentic experience you would like. An open, honest dialog of what an authentic relationship would look like to you may not only help you attain that, but your enlightening them may be a far-reaching exercise where many win.

3. Consider setting up 45-minute zoom meetings and announce at the beginning that you have a hard close at the 45-minute mark. This way you have time to stretch, refresh your water, take a bathroom break, pet your dog or go give your kid 5 minutes of love. And if you hustle, you'll have time for all of it!

Granted, we can all find a million things that need to be done in our lives if we look—just don't look and do when you have somewhere to be. Make that the focus of your attention and when you do, here is some of what you will experience:

1. You'll attend meetings with less stress, less guilt and positive energy.

2. You will be more mentally prepared for your meeting, which will promote a more productive outcome.

3. You will be un-frazzled and emotionally and physically available for

the remainder of your day. That means even making your concurring meetings on time!

4. You will feel great about not being the late one(s).

5. Not only will this way of life be habit changing, it will be a game changer in the way you live your life in relation to your self-respect, as well as your respect for others.

I'm still handing it to Meg for the work she's done on this topic over the years. She's 90% on time (progress, not perfection) and when she can't be, I hear from her, and in enough time to make alternative plans.

WRITE THIS DOWN:

1. Schedule your meetings with 15 minutes in between.

2. Try not to schedule back-to-back meetings.

3. Make a commitment to BE ON TIME 100%. Let the last-minute things you tend to do while running out the door wait until you return. Nothing will happen if they don't get done that minute, I promise. And I also promise that the benefits you'll derive from being on time will be well worth your effort and the extra time it takes to make it happen. Here's to your success...and potentially your new reputation!

WORK FROM HOME NOTES

WORK FROM HOME NOTES

WORK FROM HOME NOTES

WORK FROM HOME NOTES

Connection is why we're here.
It's what gives purpose and
meaning to our lives.

— BRENÉ BROWN

10

Communication in the Time of Corona...and Beyond

As I write this chapter while hunkered down in a friends' Airbnb, I get a text from one of my clients, Betty. From what it appears, she sounds anxious to talk to me. And while I'd love to take the break from writing, I know that any diversion is distracting, so I'm committed to staying the course. So I tell her I'll talk to her in the morning before I start day two of writing, to which she says fine.

But the more I think about it, I'd rather have that conversation with her today, so that tomorrow I can start fresh without taking the chance that my mind would be elsewhere due to our call. Betty is a client who frequently relies on me for feedback regarding communication within her team. And now that her team (a rock star team, I might add) is spread out over her city, and some even working remotely out of state, our conversations are more important than ever.

So at the end of my writing day, we hop on for a quick Zoom chat. It is there that she shares with me that after much thought and deliberation for many months, she has decided, after 24 years, to sell her business. WOW! Not what I was expecting AT ALL! I just listened as she shared her challenges, her decision-making process, and most of all, her excitement. After all, this is a challenging time for everyone. And while COVID-19, to my knowledge, hasn't directly impacted her business, it had to have at least posed some of the same questions many of us have. "What does the world now need that I have, and what is the best way to deliver that?"

The truth is, I'm delighted for her. She's worked harder than most I know to create a thriving, expanding, profitable business that employs 12 of the most engaged, collaborative, committed people I've worked with in one organization. I hope that the new firm knows how lucky they are to acquire this team, that's for sure!

Betty and I proceed to talk about how to best communicate this to the staff. Appreciating that her staff is her greatest resource, she and I consider a communication plan that will be different from the one that would have been obvious even 6 months ago—there will be no carefully crafted team gathering in the conference room!

She understands that she needs to talk to several of the directors in person, and she is willing to either meet them at the office (with masks and social distancing in place), or in one case, she agrees to meet someone outside in a local park. "How will I tell the others?" she asks. And at that moment, she realizes this is an enormously important conversation for her employees who are about to learn of a monumental change about to happen with their company. And they will receive the news in their homes without one another. This is worth working on until we get it right!

We decide on a Zoom meeting the following week, where she will tell the remainder of the staff she didn't get to in person. She will share the news, followed by an open floor to ask questions so that everyone can get off this call with as much information as they need to process. Stay tuned...

How are you communicating with your team? How are they surviving this new way of living? Have you called them individually to see how they are managing personally? And if you did it a month ago, isn't it time to do it again?

Your people are the most important asset. And just because they are out of sight is no excuse for letting them out of your mind. You might be working from your home office with a door and a window that looks out over your pool. But your people might be sharing a 1-bedroom apartment on the 22nd floor of a high-rise building, scared to death to go in the elevator just to get some fresh air, not to mention food. Everyone's reality brings different challenges, but none is less real than others.

Here's some suggestions to consider while we're working-from-home, and beyond:

1. Make it a point to reach out to your people. Whether it's your boss, your team, your family, your friends, whoever. Find out what's happening on their end, because their end looks different than yours. You might actually get a tip or two you didn't think about to manage these times.

    Meet outside when you can, if it's still not safe to go to the office. Walking and talking biz "kills two birds with one stone." Changing the atmosphere does wonders for the psyche.

    We have a bi-monthly Sunday night Zoom call with my extended family. It's big, in fact, we call it the Big Fam. We have a regular Thursday at 5 pm Zoom call with our 2 daughters to catch up and to do the *LA Times* crossword puzzle together. I Facetime my core community of women several times a week to see their face and know that they are ok. Stunning that it took this virus for us to consider what we have and to connect on a more regular basis than we ever have before.

2. Share how you like people to communicate to you during this time and beyond. I would rather get a text if someone really needs me. Then a phone call, and lastly an email. And how would you know that if I didn't tell you? My marketing partners in the UK only use What's App. And I know they'll respond quicker if I contact them that way. But I also asked them what their preference was. Don't assume anything, including that the people who you work with like the same mode of communication as you do.

3. Don't forget PTO. Now more than ever, people need to unplug. Encourage everyone on your team to do just that. Burn-out doesn't go away just because we're not cooped up in an office anymore. In fact, it tends to be worse now that so many people can't seem to draw the line between work and play.

4. Talk to your home team every day. Find out how they are. Find out what they need. Make sure they are ok and not hiding behind depression, fear, loneliness, or the many things a lockdown can reveal. Be aware of what's going on with your people, and address it when you see it.

5. On your next team Zoom meeting, invite everyone to share their top 3 silver linings from this working-from-home experience. It gets the positive energy flowing, and where energy flows, it grows. You never know: someone's silver lining might become your own. Here are just a few of the ones shared by those I've interviewed:

    ► No commute
    ► No business travel/sleep in my own bed every night
    ► More time with my husband and dog
    ► Getting more housework done

- ► More time to exercise
- ► Learning how to cook
- ► Uninterrupted work on projects (what, I want her life!)
- ► Deepened appreciation for colleagues
- ► More me-time
- ► Morning time and coffee with family
- ► Get to enjoy my home more
- ► More balanced and rested
- ► Eat healthier out of my own kitchen
- ► More time with my young child
- ► Having a home to be safe in
- ► Saving money
- ► Get laundry done during the day
- ► Deeper connections with roommates
- ► Having fun

Now, about Betty on the cusp of selling her business. You'll have to stay tuned, as I said earlier. But one thing I do know for sure: she'll communicate in a way that takes care of her people. She knows it's because of them that she has something worth selling.

WRITE THIS DOWN:

Communicate!

WORK FROM HOME NOTES

WORK FROM HOME NOTES

WORK FROM HOME NOTES

WORK FROM HOME NOTES

*And the day came when the
risk it took to remain tight in
the bud was more painful than
the risk it took to blossom.*

— ANAIS NIN

11

Conclusion

Here is the truth about my insights. While they might have started as *my* insights, *my* perspective, *my* experience and *my* reality, they are now that of hundreds of people I've either worked with, coached, or spoken to from a stage. They are tools to guide you through your work-at-home experience and beyond. And while that doesn't mean they will absolutely work in the same exact way for you, many of them just might. You get to fix what's broken and keep what is not. If you're stuck on how to get through your days with less stress and more joy, try these on for size. See how they fit on you and into your life. Practice them for a while; experience the difference that going with this flow makes. Pay close attention, and start to recognize how living with new systems makes you feel. Because, after all, doesn't it always ultimately boil down to this: How does it make you feel?

If the way you work doesn't promote satisfaction, growth or happiness, I would urge you to do something different. Remember, it's your reason, your "why," your vision of what you want this new work-from-home reality to look like that starts you on this journey to begin with. If organizing your life the way I am suggesting makes you feel better, happier, more in control, less anxious and less afraid, then great; that is what we are after!

My business and my work is ever evolving. Anyone who tells you they have not been impacted by this pandemic is lying or in major denial. Personally, professionally, spiritually, physically, emotionally, financially—pick one, hell, pick all of them. This can't not affect all of us on all levels. Yet, it's not the pandemic we are presented with, but how we choose to respond to the challenges it presents, and what we choose to do in this time of challenge that defines who we are. I choose to live in alignment with who I really am. I choose to be more conscious of my time and my experiences every single day. I choose to be purposeful and aware, to stay focused, to work hard for me and my clients, and to get more out of every minute of every day I have. Because nothing, and I mean nothing is promised, and so many good things are still possible.

I hope this book has awakened and empowered you enough to shift your thinking in the direction of action. We are all on this great adventure called life, where each of us is our own producer, executive director, and the star! We get to decide and create what we envision for ourselves and seek change as we experience moments (and pandemics), expand our thinking and learn new ways of doing things. Take control of your current circumstances. Whatever you choose to do from this moment forward, be intentional. Have your outcome in mind and be remarkable in your steadfastness to reach it.

Here's to your success, and thank you for allowing me to have with you this open and candid conversation about choices. I can't wait to find out what you've chosen.

A few of my silver linings:

▶ I wrote a book!

▶ I spend more time with Marty and Ruby

▶ I see my girls on Zoom every Thursday

▶ I see my Big Fam every other Sunday night

▶ I'm seeing my community more virtually than I did in person

▶ I'm helping clients set up their work-from-home space

▶ I'm helping clients learn how to rock the virtual webinar stage

▶ I spend no time at the airport or anticipating travel delays

▶ I work out on my driveway every week

▶ We got an indoor bike (busting my A**)

▶ I started doing crossword puzzles, which challenge my brain and keep me young

▶ I stopped dying my hair—eau natural is da bomb!

▶ I'm painting rocks with inspirational words and spreading them all over the neighborhood

WORK FROM HOME NOTES

WORK FROM HOME NOTES

WORK FROM HOME NOTES

WORK FROM HOME NOTES

The change is in the
CHOOSING.

— WENDY ELLIN

12

Tools & Checklists

Morning Routine Tools & Checklist:

- ☐ R.P.M. (Rise. Pee. Meditate)

- ☐ Insight Timer App

- ☐ Hydrate

- ☐ Move Your Body

- ☐ Gratitude Journal

- ☐ Assess Your Day

- ☐ Get to Your M.I.T.s

Declutter/Office Creation Tools & Checklist:

- ☐ 3-Box Process in every space

- ☐ Keep "to do" and "to save" items

☐ Create permanent homes for everything

☐ Only keep what you NEED and LOVE

☐ "Use it or Lose it" Box

☐ Scope out the best space to set up home office

☐ Writing desk/Amazon

☐ Screen to create division in room/Amazon

Paper Organizing Tools & Checklist:

☐ Command Central File for TO DOs

☐ File drawer or bin/box

☐ Hanging folders

☐ 3-½ inch clear plastic tabs

☐ Label maker/label tape

☐ Colored stickers

☐ 3x5 index cards

☐ A-Z reference file for TO SAVE'S

☐ Make 1 of 5 choices

Email Decluttering Tools & Checklist:

☐ Sort by sender

☐ Round 1: Delete what you don't need

☐ Round 2: Create subject or person folders

- ☐ Round 3: _ COMMAND CENTRAL

  - ☐ _ACTION THIS WEEK

  - ☐ _NO DEADLINE

  - ☐ _AWAITING RESPONSE

  - ☐ _AWAITING TO READ

- ☐ Numbered folders for main categories in inbox

- ☐ Subfolders under them

Desktop Tools & Checklist:

- ☐ Create one folder with your name/initials on it

- ☐ Inside that folder lives subfolders with subjects

- ☐ Sub-folders live in those.

iPhone Home Page Tools & Checklist:

- ☐ Create folders on home page by color

- ☐ Drag apps according to their color into designated folders

- ☐ All apps/color folders will remain on home page

Managing Your Home Team:

- ☐ White board

- ☐ Platform for laptop if needed to create adequate height for Zoom calls

- ☐ Ring light for better lighting for zoom calls

- ☐ Second screen/monitor to work with

- ☐ Red light bulb on desk lamp

- ☐ Outlets for technology

- ☐ Timer

- ☐ *Please Do Not Disturb* sign

Procrastination, Perfectionism, and Workaholism Tools & Checklist:

- ☐ Start the project, one small part at a time

- ☐ Put the start date on the calendar and honor it

- ☐ Schedule things on your calendar to get you away from your work

- ☐ Replace perfect with great, and let that be good enough

Being on Time Tools & Checklist:

- ☐ End Zoom meetings at the 45-minute mark to create breaks in between meetings

- ☐ Get on 5 minutes and keep your audio/video off until it starts

- ☐ Change your mind set about timeliness—late is not an option!

Communication Tools & Checklist:

- ☐ Talk to your people, all of them

- ☐ Put it in your calendar to check in on everyone regularly

- ☐ Listen to what your people need, both your Home Team and your Work Team

- ☐ Remind your employees of PTO—everyone needs it and deserves it

- ☐ Have Zoom social calls as well as work calls

- ☐ Share how you want to be communicated to

So, here we are, at the end of our journey together. Yet, at the beginning of what you get to as you implement these tools and strategies into your daily reality. Now's your time. Now's your opportunity to set up your work-from-home space so that even if/when we transition to some kind of hybrid office/home work situation, you will have figured it out, stuck with it long enough to reap the benefits, and are ROCKING your productivity.

You got this. And I'm with you, both in spirit, and in real time all along the way. Just reach out to me at wendy@wendyellin.com and let me know all of it: your challenges, your successes, your "aha" moments, your mess ups, your redo's, your before and after pics, your ideas I haven't even thought of - I'm open and available to hearing all of it.

And if you think you need more help, please ask for it. Just because you've lived a certain way your entire life doesn't mean you have to remain stuck. Unless you want to be. It's your choice. Make one that serves you well. Make one that aligns with who you are as a person, as a parent, as a partner, and as a professional. You, and the entire world, will be so much better, and thrive so much fuller because of it.